Amsterdam

Mini **Visitors'** Guide

Amsterdam Mini Visitors' Guide
ISBN – 978-9948-03-444-5

Copyright © Explorer Group Ltd 2008
All rights reserved.

All maps © Explorer Group Ltd 2008

Front cover photograph: Tim Binks

Printed and bound by
Emirates Printing Press, Dubai, UAE

Explorer Publishing & Distribution
PO Box 34275, Dubai, United Arab Emirates
Phone (+971 4) 340 8805
Fax (+971 4) 340 8806
Email info@explorerpublishing.com
Web www.explorerpublishing.com

Welcome to the *Amsterdam Mini Visitors'
Guide*. This mini marvel, perfect for visitors,
is brought to you by the same team behind
the *Amsterdam Complete Residents' Guide*.
Written entirely by Amsterdam locals, this
guide includes everything from the most
interesting museums and galleries to the
best places to shop and Amsterdam's finest
restaurants, cafes and bars. If you want to
know more about Explorer Publishing, or
tell us anything that we've missed, go to
www.explorerpublishing.com.

Amsterdam Mini Visitors' Guide

Editorial Team: Tim Binks, Richard Greig, Grace Carnay
Designers: Rafi VP, Shawn Jackson Zuzarte
Contributing Editor: Ann Maher
Authors: Andy Baker, Ann Maher, Cindy Yianni, Elise Krentzel,
Jane Stephenson, Kim Chandler, Prue Duggan
Photographers: Victor Romero, Tim Binks, Pamela Grist

Contents

Essentials

Alluring Amsterdam

With outstanding culture, stunning architecture, cosy bars and edgier delights, this charming, cosmopolitan city has it all. Welcome to Amsterdam.

Artists, students, rebels and renegades have always been attracted to Amsterdam, a cosmopolitan capital famed for its tolerance. They still come in their droves (176 nationalities live here) but the city has as many facets as one of its sparkly diamonds. Famous in some circles and infamous in others, it is a well-known destination for both the party crowd and culture lovers, but visitors are still surprised how much it has to offer aside from coffeeshops and the Red Light District. It's an extraordinarily relaxing city that is a joy to walk around.

Its small scale is enormously appealing and it has very few boring, civic institutional type buildings (they're in Den Haag). Its main pleasures lie in domestic architecture and detail. Floating houseboats, hidden hofjes, the stone slab on a 17th century house denoting the trade of its first owner. There's something interesting to see around every corner and each neighbourhood has its own distinctive atmosphere and cafes.

And there always seems to be time for a coffee or a beer. Don't these people have jobs to go to? Of course. The Dutch economy is strong; Amsterdam is a highly sought after business destination and a hotspot for those working in the creative and media industries. But Amsterdammers definitely work to live. The arts are taken seriously (but are there for everyone, not the elite) with a multitude of museums, 40

The area in front of Centraal Station

concerts every day, original and creative festivals in the summer and a legendary party scene. Annual events such as New Year, Queen's Day and Sinterklaas are celebrated with exuberance and everyone joins in. There are pleasures in every season. Cold, wet and dark in winter with mist hanging over the canals, this is the time for comfort food and split pea soup – the cold weather staple. If you visit in the spring, a trip to the bulb fields is obligatory, while in the summer the city explodes with people sitting on the romantic terraces along the tree-lined canals, sunning themselves in the Vondelpark, or pottering about in small boats on the canals.

Recent years have seen the city authorities embark on a major refurbishment of Amsterdam and the city has continued to expand and grow, across the IJ in Amsterdam Noord, along the south-east axis, and most strikingly in the docklands and harbour area behind Centraal Station. This modern architecture acts as a counterpoint to the Disney-esque cuteness of the city centre.

Amsterdam Checklist

01 Cruise The Canals

Glide past Golden Age mansions shimmering in the sunshine on a hot summer's day, or under bridges twinkling with hundreds of fairy lights at night. Combine a cruise with culture on the museum boat, but you must see the city from the water. See p.111.

02 Get Out Of Town By Bike

Cycling in town is interesting, but for the best scenery, head out to the country. In half an hour you can be cycling along the beautiful Amstel or around one of the Waterland villages north of Amsterdam. See Further Out (p.100) or Bicycle Tours (p.110).

03 Wander In Circles

As you wander Amsterdam's intimate streets and
canals, you may find yourself heading in a different
direction to the way you thought you were heading.
Walking in circles? Not exactly, but enjoy it. If you
want to shorten your walk, head for the centre.

04 Eat Frites

Dutch frites are worth seeking out. The best are the Vlaamse (Flemish) frites – and you'll get lots of sauce for dunking. Choose from mayonnaise, ketchup, curry ketchup, satay sauce and chopped raw onions. Or have the lot! To find out where to try them, see p.225.

05 Catch A Concert

Classical music isn't elitist in this town – everyone can enjoy the amazing acoustics of the Concertgebouw for free at one of the popular Wednesday lunchtime concerts. For contemporary sounds, head for Melkweg or Paradiso. See p.218.

06 Browse The Markets

Amsterdammers flock to the city's markets. Albert Cuypstraat Markt (p.148) is the biggest, with something for everyone. Waterlooplein (p.151) is popular with tourists. Locals prefer Dapperstraat (p.149), while the fashionistas' favourite is Noordermarkt (p.150).

07 Go Dutch

The brown cafe (p.167) is Amsterdam at its most gezellig (cosy, warm, comforting). Head for Jordaan and get ready to while away hours and hours, just like the locals. There are some super-scenic venues on the Brouwersgracht (see p.72).

08 View The City's Skyline

Club 11 (p.181), at the top of the Post-CS building near Centraal Station, has been a star since it opened. A great place for a cocktail or to cut loose at the weekend, it's also open for lunch and dinner every day, and has fantastic views out over the city.

09 Hunt For Hofjes

These almshouses with their courtyards and gardens are little oases in the bustling city. The Begijnhof (p.65) off Spui is the best known, but there are lots in the Jordaan (p.72). That little doorway in the ivy-clad wall may lead somewhere wonderful.

10 See The Tulips In Bloom

When it's spring, the world descends on Keukenhof (p.102) and the bulb-growing area of the Netherlands to gasp at amazing colours in field after field of tulips and other blooms laid out like Mondriaan paintings. Visit before the flowers are beheaded!

Best Of Amsterdam

For Budget Travellers

You don't need to stay at The Grand to enjoy Amsterdam, but you will need to move fast, as anything cheap and charming goes quick. The StayOkay chain (p.55) is deservedly popular; designer options include the Qbic (p.53). There are also hostels and campsites (p.55). For cheap eats, head for De Pijp (p.196) and feast on spicy Surinamese and other multicultural treats, or stock up for a picnic at Albert Cuypmarkt (p.148) or Noordermarkt (p.150). Many highlights can be enjoyed for free: take a ferry across the IJ to see the city from the water, sample some culture at Amsterdams Historisch Museum (p.65), or see a Wednesday lunchtime performance at the Concertgebouw (p.219). And just wander: the incomparable views cost nothing.

For Short Stays

Amsterdam is such an intimate city that one weekend is enough to cram in culture, shopping, a trip to the countryside, and still leave time to linger over a beer in a snug brown cafe in Jordaan (p.184) or a glass of rose on a sunny terrace. Book tickets online to jump the queues at Rijksmuseum (p.83) and Van Gogh Museum (p.84) and leave time for browsing around the tempting shops of the Negen Straatjes (p.146). Get a taste of Golden Age life in a canal-side house such as Museum Van Loon (p.72). If the weather is fine, hire a bike to explore Broek-in-Waterland, Oudekerk aan de Amstel or the eastern docklands. If it is raining, well, there are over 30 museums in Amsterdam or maybe another biertje…?

For Families

The city's dinky scale is very appealing to children and Dutch life is family oriented, with kids welcome pretty much everywhere. You can't go wrong with a boat trip (p.26), or for the energetic, a canal bike (p.114). Artis Zoo (p.89) and Vondelpark (p.85) are top destinations for when the sun's shining. If it's raining, underground playground-in-a-carpark TunFun (p.26) is great for letting off steam and the Van Gogh (p.84) and Rijksmuseum (p.83) collections are nicely concise. For older children, Anne Frank Huis (p.73) is fascinating, followed by a climb up the tower next door at Westerkerk (p.77). Most kids will also race up the ladders of the working windmills at Zaanse Schans (p.102), an accessible half hour from Amsterdam.

For Big Spenders

For sheer drama and fantastic location, The Dylan Hotel (p.50) takes some beating if money is no limit, although the enchanting elegance of The Grand (p.51) has many fans and the staff to guest ratio at the InterContinental Amstel (p.50) means all whims are catered for. For culinary adventures you can't aim higher than the 23rd floor of the Okura hotel and Ciel Bleu (p.200) with its two Michelin stars. Ron Blaauw (p.190) also has two and Yamazato (p.203) one. Shopping opportunities for fine art and collectibles abound in the Spiegelquartier (p.147). In Oud Zuid (p.142) there are lots of smart shopping opportunities alongside well-heeled locals. But for something really flashy, cop a rock and buy a diamond.

Visiting Amsterdam

Flights to Amsterdam, one of Europe's main hubs for air travel, are common. Fast, regular train links get you into the city easily.

Getting There

There are direct flights connecting Amsterdam to all major cities of the world. A hundred airlines fly into Schiphol Airport (see below) of which a quarter are budget airlines that fly to the Netherlands from the UK and Ireland, eastern and western Europe and Scandinavia. The national airline is KLM, which merged with Air France in 2004 to form the largest airline group in the world, servicing 250 destinations.

With the opening of the high-speed rail link in St Pancras Station London, it is possible to travel at up to 186 miles per hour from London to Amsterdam (changing at Brussels). Total journey time: five and a half hours.

Schiphol Airport

Schiphol is a sleek, highly efficient airport used by 40 million passengers each year (www.schiphol.nl). There is one terminal building, and commercial activity is centred around Schiphol Plaza, with lots of shopping and duty free, a communication centre in departure lounges one and two, and Wi-Fi in several locations (and roaming), although you have to pay for this facility. First aid and emergency medical care is available 24 hours a day, seven days a week and is

Horses hauling Heineken

provided by Airport Medical Services (above departure hall two). The number for lost property is 0900 0141.

From The Airport

By train it takes 15 minutes from Schiphol to Centraal Station (30 minutes to Den Haag and an hour to Rotterdam). There are six trains an hour from 06:00 to 01:00, then one an hour through the night. Buy tickets (€3.60) at the yellow machines in the baggage hall and plaza, with cash (coins only) or plastic.

Some hotels provide their own free shuttle bus from the airport or there's the Connexxion hotel shuttle bus (038 339 47 41) that services 100 hotels. It runs every 10 minutes or so from 06:00 to 21:00 and the fee is €11 one way. You don't have to be staying at a hotel to use it. Taxis are available at the rank outside. The fare to the city centre (14 kilometres away) is approximately €40.

Airlines

Air France	020 654 57 20	www.airfrance.com
BMI	020 346 92 11	www.flybmi.com
British Airways	020 346 95 59	www.ba.com
Cathay Pacific	020 653 20 10	www.cathaypacific.com
Continental Airlines	020 346 93 81	www.continental.com
easyJet	0900 265 8022	www.easyjet.com
KLM	020 474 77 47	www.klm.com
Lufthansa	0900 123 4777	www.lufthansa.com
Singapore Airlines	020 548 88 88	www.singaporeair.com
Transavia	0900 0737	www.transavia.com

Visas

The length of your stay, the purpose of your visit and your nationality (ie the documents you are travelling with, if you have dual nationality) are the factors determining visa requirements. Citizens from the EU, North America and Australasia, for example, generally only need a valid passport for a stay of three months or less. Contact your own embassy for details or see the Dutch Ministry for Foreign Affairs website (www.minbuza.nl) – under 'Coming to the Netherlands: When You Require a Visa' – which lists which countries need what.

The Netherlands is one of the 15 countries in the Schengen area where a visa to one country enables free movement through the other 14. The scheme, set up in 1995, is designed to simplify border crossings and immigration control. The tourist visa (C-Visa) issued by the Netherlands is usually a Schengen Visa, but again, it is always worth checking with your own embassy. The visa will usually only be valid for a maximum of three months. For further information see www.schengen.com.

Customs

What you can bring in and take out, and other information related to

---

i Checking In

Self-service check-in is available for 25 airlines in departure halls one, two and three. Baggage allowances vary between airlines – some go by pieces, some by weight. Many budget airlines are now charging passengers for checked-in luggage. As a major international hub, security checks, and the queues for them, can be lengthy.

reclaimable taxes and restrictions can be found on the customs website (www.duane.nl). If you are coming from another EU country, there's generally no restrictions on most goods, provided they are for your own use and you have already paid any due taxes where you bought them.

Alcohol and tobacco have limits, but you'll have a struggle getting 110 litres of beer and 800 cigarettes into your pull-along. Other restricted or banned items include flowers, plants and fruit, drugs and medicines and artwork. Stricter rules apply when you are entering the Netherlands from a country outside the EU. Non-EU travellers that purchase goods in Amsterdam and are entitled to a VAT refund, can have their VAT paid out in cash at Schiphol, but keep all your receipts and don't check in the relevant goods before seeing customs in Departures 3.

Visitor Information

The VVV (www.vvv.amsterdam.nl) is the organisation for visitors and tourists in the Netherlands and they have outposts all over the country. In Amsterdam, there are two offices at Centraal Station and one at Leidseplein (see below), and one at Schiphol Airport. There are a wide range of brochures, maps and guides for sale and (for a fee) they can also book

Tourist Information		
VVV Centraal Station	Stationsplein Perron 2B 15, Centrum	020 551 25 25
VVV Leidsestraat	Leidseplein 1, Canal Belt	020 551 25 25
VVV Stationsplein	Stationsplein 10, Centrum	020 551 25 25

Crowds on Damrak on Queen's Day

accommodation. You can sometimes get a good deal if you do this because hotels submit a daily rate each morning that fluctuates wildly depending on individual hotel occupancy.

The ANWB (the Dutch Automobile Association) is a very useful source of (mostly Dutch) guides and maps for cyclists and car users, with some useful route-planning and distance calculators. The city websites www.amsterdamtourist.nl and www.iamsterdam.nl provide masses of information and tips for visitors and residents. In addition to these 'official' sources, there are innumerable directories and web-based guides about the city, catering for the interests of every type of visitor (see p.33). If you want to explore other regions of the country outside Amsterdam, the website www.holland.com is an extremely useful starting point.

Local Knowledge

Climate

Amsterdam has a temperate climate characterised by mild winters, cool summers, and year-round precipitation (averaging 60-80cm per month), so come prepared for rain in every season. Winters (1-4°C) can be windy, spring (6-11°C) delightful, summers (14-19°C) can get hot and humid, with active mosquitoes and spectacular thunderstorms, but autumn (9-13°C) is quieter.

Crime & Safety

Amsterdam is a comfortably safe city – just take sensible precautions. Watch your wallet, backpack and laptop on the train from the airport. Don't carry a camera in the Red Light District. Leave nothing in your car, not even the boot: 'Niets er in... Niets er uit' (nothing in, nothing out) is the police advice. The Amsterdam Tourist Assistance Service (ATAS) at 104-108 Nieuwezijds Voorburgwal (10:00 to 22:00) provides practical support and help for tourist who are victims of crime.

Dos & Don'ts

Don't buy drugs, bikes or hotel rooms from strangers on the street. Don't smoke a joint anywhere except inside a coffeeshop. Don't take photos in the Red Light District. Don't walk in the bike lane. If you are on a bike, watch out for pedestrians and tramlines and lock up your bike at all times.

Do enjoy Amsterdam for free: an architectural tour, a picnic in Vondelpark, a ferry trip across the IJ or a free concert at the Concertgebouw or Boekmanzaal. Get out of Amsterdam to visit castles, beaches and the masterpieces of hydraulic engineering that keep the water out – everything is so near. Just act normal, because that's mad enough! (popular Dutch saying).

Electricity

The voltage in Holland is 230 volts. In hotels, you may find a 110-volt or 120-volt shaver connection. If in doubt, bring a power converter and adapter for two-prong, round-prong plugs with side grounding contacts.

Gay & Lesbian

Amsterdam is one of the gay capitals of the world. There is no West Village like in New York City or Old Compton Street in London, but there are pink zones in the centre such as the bars on the Reguliersdwarsstrat. All are fairly mixed as far as race and nationality are concerned – even Habibi Ana (p.194), possibly the only Arabic gay bar in the world. For more on Gay & Lesbian venues for going out, see p.182.

Sites to visit include the Homomonument (Westermarkt, Jordaan), where pink triangles commemorate the gay men and women who lost their lives during the second world war, and Het Mandje at the Amsterdamse Historiche Museum (p.65), a brilliant reconstruction of the legendary gay bar opened in 1927 by its owner, lesbian biker chick Bet van Beeren.

Homosexual rights are enshrined in law: civil unions for same sex couples became legal in 1998, and in 2001 Mayor Job Cohen officiated over the world's first same-sex marriages that offered full civil rights.

There are a few annual celebrations organised for and by the gay community. Rozezaterdag (www.rozezaterdag.nl), or Pink Saturday, is held in June in a different city every year. Amsterdam Gay Pride (p.37) is held in August and is one of the city's biggest events. There is also a fairly large Leather Pride Amsterdam festival, usually held in November.

For more information, check out www.gayamsterdam. com – a top portal including a hotel guide, www.coc.nl – the oldest gay, lesbian, bisexual, and transgender organisation in the world, and www.pinkpoint.nl – a gay and lesbian information kiosk by the Homomonument.

Kids

Amsterdam is a great city for smaller explorers. A boat trip (p.111), of some kind, is a must. Hire a canal bike, go on a tourist cruise or take one of the free ferries that go back and forth to Amsterdam Noord (behind Centraal Station). When it's raining, TunFun Speelpark is an enormous underground playground fashioned out of a multi-storey carpark. Top 'educational' stops include interactive Science Center NEMO (p.95), housed in a giant, green ship with the replica Dutch East India Company (VOC) ship currently moored outside.

Art lovers will enjoy the Van Gogh Museum (p.84), with a terrific audio guide for children. Free entertainment can be found at numerous parks and playgrounds with cuddly animals at petting zoos (kinderboerderijen, p.116), and wilder beasts in the excellent Artis Zoo (p.89). Toasted sandwiches (available everywhere), pancakes and poffertjes (puffed up smaller versions) are top scoff. Outside Amsterdam, top attractions include the Efteling theme park (www.efteling.nl), Space Expo at Noordwijk (0900 8765 4321), or miles of windy coastline (see Seaside & Islands on p.104). Hotels can sometimes provide babysitting (using agencies such as Oppascentrale).

Language
Dutch is the official language, but everyone speaks brilliant English in Amsterdam. The clicky, guttural sound of Dutch is pretty difficult to get the hang of, but even the smallest effort will be appreciated and respected. See Basic Dutch on p.28.

Lost & Found
Lost and found objects are sent (from police stations) to the lost and found bureau (Bureau Gevonden Voorwerpen, 020 559 30 05) once a day. If you lose something at Schiphol

Emergency numbers

American Express (Stolen cards)	020 504 8666
ATAS (Tourist assistance)	020 625 3246
Chemist/Pharmacy helpline	0900 7244 7465
Dentist (Tandartsen)	0900 821 2230
Diners Club (Stolen cards)	020 654 5511
Doctors (Huizarten)	020 592 3434
Fire, police and ambulance	112
Lost & Found Bureau	020 559 3005
MasterCard/Eurocard (Stolen cards)	030 283 5555
Road Patrol ANWB	0800 0888
SOS (24 hour helpline)	020 675 7575
STD Clinic	020 555 5822
Visa (Stolen cards)	0800 022 3110

Basic Dutch

General	
Good morning	Goedemorgen
Hello/good day	Dag/goedendag
Goodbye	Dag
See you later	Tot ziens!
Yes	Ja
No	Nee
Please	Alstublieft
Thank you	Dank u
You're welcome	Graag gedaan
Sorry	Sorry

Questions	
How much...?	Wat kost...?
Where	Waar
When	Wanneer
Which	Welk(e)
Who	Wie
Why	Waarom
What	Wat

Emergency	
Accident	Ongeluk
I am ill	Ik ben ziek
Doctor	Dokter
Police	Politie

Directions	
Street	Straat
Close to	Vlakbij
Beach	Strand
Airport	Luchthaven
Bank	Bank
Straight ahead	Rechtdoor
Right	Rechts
Left	Links
Stop	Stop

Numbers	
One	Een
Two	Twee
Three	Drie
Four	Vier
Five	Vijf
Six	Zes
Seven	Zeven
Eight	Acht
Nine	Negen
Ten	Tien
Twenty	Twintig
Thirty	Dertig
Fifty	Vijftig
Hundred	Honderd

phone 0900 0141 or +31 (0)20 794 0800 from abroad, or e-mail the form from the website (www.schiphol.com). There is a €5 administration fee for each item when you pick it up.

Money

The Netherlands has had the euro (€) since 2002. Note denominations are €5, €10, €20, €50, €100, €200 and €500 euros, but you may have problems using anything bigger than a €50. Coins come in €2, €1, 50 cents, 20 cents, 10 cents and 5 cents. The one and two cent coins remain legal tender, but are no longer issued. Sums are rounded to the nearest five cents.

All major credit cards are widely accepted in hotels and restaurants, but not in supermarkets, bars or cafes. You may have to pay a few cents more if you want to use the card for transactions under a certain threshold.

ATMs are widely available (including in some supermarkets) ,in several languages, and they dispense money 24 hours a day. A wide range of cards are accepted. Banks are generally open Tuesday to Friday, 09:00 to 16:00, and on Mondays from 13:00, although some have longer hours.

To change money, exchanges in hotels and banks generally offer poor rates (except Postbank). Shop around among the myriad of small exchanges in the tourist centre. The GWK Travelex offices (11 branches) are worth trying (www.travelex.com, 0900 0566).

People With Disabilities

With its narrow uneven streets and bicycles parked everywhere, Amsterdam isn't brilliant terrain for people with physical disabilities, although once you are at a museum, for example, it should be fine. Help is available for getting to and through the airport (see www.ihd-schiphol.nl), and in the city the newer trams have low central doors accessible by wheelchair. The metro is also accessible. For more information contact the Bureau for Disabled Travellers (Bureau Assistentieverlening Gehandicapten) on 030 235 78 22.

Police
There is a significant police presence in town, especially in tourist hotspots such as the Red Light District, as well as 4,000 uniformed 'town watchers' on patrol and 2,000 volunteers who have the same training as regular police officers.

Postal Services
The main post office is located on Singel 250 and is open from 09:00 to 18:00 weekdays, and till 15:00 on Saturdays. Use the 'overige' postcodes slot in letterboxes for your postcards home. There are other smaller Postbanks where you can buy stamps, postcards and dispatch small parcels.

Public Toilets
Apart from some at Centraal Station, the iron green pissoirs for men, and the odd one or two dotted about town, you should head for cafes, restaurants, hotels, department stores, museums and other tourist sites. You'll often have to pay 25 cents or so to a rather fierce matron guarding the facilities, and if you're lucky, you'll be (reluctantly) allowed to choose from a box of sweets.

Telephone & Internet

You can make international calls from public telephones using a phone card (available from station bookshops and post offices) or a credit card. Mobile coverage is good. For the internet, there are around 200 hotspots in the city, with good Wi-Fi in hotels and cafes. A number of internet cafes can be found in the centre, or you can surf for free (with a fantastic view) at Amsterdam's new library by the Post-CS building.

Time

Local time is one hour ahead of Coordinated Universal Time, formerly GMT (UTC+1). The Netherlands also use Central European Summer Time, for which clocks go forward one hour on the last Sunday in March (to UTC+2), then go back again on the last Sunday in October (returning to UTC+1).

Tipping

Tax and service charges are included in bills for everything – from restaurant meals to taxis – but tipping is common, even if only a little extra rounding up to the nearest appropriate unit. Salaries for waiting staff are good enough to live on, so it's more a question of manners or appreciation of good service.

Women

Women travelling alone will not feel uncomfortable in Amsterdam. But solo exploration of the seedier parts of town at night, such as the Red Light District, is not advisable. It's just common sense really.

Media & Further Reading

Newspapers & Magazines

English language and international newspapers are widely available on the day of publication. They are more expensive than at 'home' and some international editions have fewer pages. Local English-language press includes award-winning cultural paper *Amsterdam Weekly*, the more news-oriented *The Times,* and monthly *Roundabout*.

Television & Radio

Most hotels have cable, which includes BBC channels, CNN and Eurosport. Local Amsterdam channel AT5 (www.at5.nl) is fun: Mayor Job Cohen pops in on Thursdays to chat about his week. Radio Netherlands (www.radionetherlands.nl) offers some interesting programming in English.

Books

Amsterdam is well covered in books of all kinds. Cultural guides include *The Undutchables* by Colin White, *Dealing with the Dutch* by Jacob Vossestein and *The Dutch I Presume* by Martijn de Rooi. Locally published books include the food guide *Delicious Amsterdam* by Johannes van Dam and smaller explorers will love *The Cow That Fell in the Canal* by Phyllis Krasilovsky.

Amsterdam appears in fiction in John Irving's *Widow for One Year*, *The Acid House* by Irvine Welsh and *Amsterdam* by Geert Mak. For a dazzling look at the Golden Age, *The Embarrassment of Riches* by Simon Schama is a racy read. Anna Pavord's *The Tulip* and Deborah Moggach's *Tulip Fever* give fascinating insights into the famous bloom. If you can find a copy, William Hoffman's *Queen Juliana: The Story of the*

Richest Woman in the World (she wasn't) is a colourful account of the origins of the Dutch royal family.

Recent events are tackled in *The Death of Theo van Gogh and the Limits of Tolerance* by Ian Buruma, and *Infidel* by Ayaan Hirsi Ali. *Brilliant Orange* by David Winner is a great read even if you know nothing about Cruyff or 'total football'. Anyone looking to relocate to Amsterdam should pick up a copy of the *Amsterdam Complete Residents' Guide*, which includes everything you need to know about your new city.

Useful Websites

There's no shortage of websites about Amsterdam, starting with the city's official sites, and plenty of unoffical ones.

Websites	
www.amsterdam.info.nl	Useful info and local links
www.amsterdamtourist.com	Unofficial Amsterdam site
www.amsterdamtourist.nl	The official tourist board site
www.channels.nl	Virtual Amsterdam tours
www.coolcapitals.nl	Groovy site with cute graphics
www.holland.com	Official Netherlands tourist board site
www.iamsterdam.com	The official Amsterdam site
www.maps.google.nl	Detailed maps of the Netherlands
www.simplyamsterdam.nl	Useful info and local links
www.goudengids.nl	Yellow Pages
www.hetweer.nl	The weather
www.iens.nl	Restaurant reviews
www.weekendhotel.nl	Cool hotels and B&Bs

New Year is spectacular, Queen's Day a riot of orange, and watch out for flying ginger biscuits during Sinterklaas.

Public Holidays

The Dutch celebrate festivals and holidays exuberantly, and they are marked with ceremonies and celebrations throughout the country. On public holidays, banks and public offices will be closed or open shorter hours, but shops and museum hours vary widely, so it's wise to check before you go. The Netherlands is unusual in having two days to commemorate the second world war: 4 May is a solemn day of remembrance, while 5 May is a celebration to mark liberation from occupation.

From the middle of November until 5 December, Sinterklaas (Feast of St Nicholas) is huge, with nightly TV bulletins (Sint's horse generally goes missing), and extravagant decorations everywhere. But the biggest one is Queen's Day, a riotous national holiday to celebrate the Queen's birthday.

Public Holidays	2008
New Year's Day (Nieuwjaar)	1 January
Easter (Pasen)	23/24 March
Queen's Day (Koninginnedag)	30 April
Ascension (Hemelvaart)	1 May
Whitsun (Pinksteren)	11/12 May
Christmas Day (Kerstmis)	25/26 December

34

Annual Events

Amsterdam Boat Show

March

Amsterdam RAI, Buitenveldert
www.hiswa.nl

Annual boat show at the Amsterdam RAI Exhibition Centre, with hundreds of boats, yachts and accessories.

Stille Omgang

March

Various Locations
www.stille-omgang.nl

A silent Catholic procession to commemorate the 1345 Miracle of Amsterdam, held between midnight and 04:00.

Amsterdam Fantastic Film Festival

April

Various Locations
www.afff.nl

A cult annual institution with screenings of European and international thriller, cult, horror and science-fiction movies.

National Museum Weekend

April

Various Locations
www.museumweekend.nl

A weekend when over 450 museums throughout the country open for free (or at least a reduced price). There are also many special events, but some of the museums get very crowded.

Queen's Day (Koninginnedag)

April

Various Locations
www.koninginnedagamsterdam.nl

The big one. A chaotic and vibrant mix of street party, festival and flea market when for one day only there is a 'free market' (vrijmarkt), enabling anyone to set up a stall and sell a stupendous variety of junk. Orangeness is everywhere.

Liberation Day
May

Various Locations
www.4en5mei.nl

Commemorating the liberation of Holland from its Nazi occupiers in 1945, the city holds a ceremony in Dam Square.

National Windmill Day
May

Various Locations
www.molens.nl

1,000 windmills open to the public, with top 'molen' spotting at Kinderdijk and Zaanse Schans. See website for other locations.

Amsterdam Roots Festival
June

Various Locations
www.amsterdamroots.nl

A week of world music at venues such as Paradiso, Melkweg and De Balie, with some outside events at the Oosterpark.

Holland Festival
June

Various Locations
www.hollandfestival.nl

Internationally acclaimed month-long festival of opera, dance, music, film and art in venues all over Amsterdam.

Open Garden Days
June

Various Locations
www.grachtenmusea.nl

Discover the beautiful gardens that lie behind the stately facades of Amsterdam's canal-side homes.

Amsterdam Fashion Week
July

Various Locations
www.amsterdamfashionweek.com

Winter and Spring events for lowland fashionistas. 100 venues participate in fashion shows, launches, events and parties.

Dance Valley
Spaarnwoude

July

www.dancevalley.nl

The biggest and most popular open-air dance event held in the Netherlands, regularly attracting 45,000 visitors.

Over 't IJ Festival
North Amsterdam

July

www.overhetij.nl

The world is a stage, but so is an old factory, a shipping container, a boat or a Russian submarine, in this eclectic cultural event in North Amsterdam.

Kwakoe Festival
Bijlmerpark

July/August

www.kwakoe.nl

The Netherlands' biggest multicultural festival, which focuses on the Suriname, Antillean and African communities and cultures. Events, held every weekend, offer live music, dance, performances, parties, literature, sport and food.

De Parade
Martin Luther Kingpark, Amstel

August & December

www.deparade.nl

A unique travelling theatre festival with tents, a roundabout, world restaurants and a variety of shows every night.

Amsterdam Gay Pride
Various Locations

August

www.amsterdamgaypride.nl

One of the biggest gay and lesbian events in Europe featuring an extravagant canal parade with 100 lavishly decorated boats on the Prinsengracht, attracting 250,000 spectators each year. One of Amsterdam's busiest weekends.

Grachtenfestival
Various Locations

August

www.grachtenfestival.nl

A truly magical event, with nine days of classical performances taking place on a pontoon outside the Hotel Pulitzer.

Open Monumentendag
Various Locations

September

www.openmonumentendag.nl

Thousands of historically and architecturally significant monuments and sites are open to the public, free of charge.

Robodock
Various Locations

September

www.robodock.nl

A thrilling, unpredictable combination of theatre, drama, acrobatics, art, robots, fire and water in NDSM.

Amsterdam Marathon
Through Amsterdam

October

www.ingamsterdammarathon.nl

25,000 runners take the long way round Amsterdam.

High Times Cannabis Cup
Various Locations

November

www.Cannabis.Cup

An annual event for marijuana aficionados – get a judge's pass (€200) for admission to all the ceremonies and events.

Museumnacht
Various Locations

November

www.n8.nl

Amsterdam's museums open their doors to the public from 19:00 on Friday to 02:00 on Saturday morning, with DJs, dancing, music and food alongside the permanent collections.

From left: Queen's Day on the canals, the Drag Queen Olympics

Sinterklaas
November/December

Various Locations | www.sinterklaas.nl

From the middle of November until Pakjesavonds (Presents Night) on 5 December, the Dutch go Sinterklaas mad. Poems, chocolate letters, presents left in shoes and trillions of ginger biscuits (pepernoten) flying in all directions.

New Year's Eve
December

A particularly raucous affair involving stupendous quantities of fireworks and firecrackers, let off in scarily uncontrolled environments (like right in front of you).

Getting Around

Amsterdam is a compact city and easy to get around. Explore by bus, train, tram, ferry or (of course) by bicycle.

Public transport in Amsterdam is safe, reliable and cheap. Buses and trams (the best ways to get around) and the metro use a one ticket system, the 'strippenkart'. A full fare 15 strip strippenkart is €6.80 (travel within the city centre is one zone or two strips) and a 45 strip version is €20.10. This system is due to be replaced in January 2009 by the ov-chipkaart (PT Smart Card) that is currently available just for the metro.

The GVB is Amsterdam's public transport body and its website (www.gvb.nl) includes maps, ticket information, timetables and routes. 24, 48, 72 and 96 hour discount passes can be bought at the office opposite Centraal Station. Trains are good for journeys out of town. The city is less convenient for motorists – parking is limited, drivers need to be constantly aware of bicycles and straying tourists, and traffic is heavy. Taxis are expensive, but bicycles are a great way to see the city.

Boat

There is no shortage of water-borne transport options for sauntering around Amsterdam's 165 canals and other waterways. Tourist-focused transport includes 110 glass-topped canal boats (see Boat Tours on p.111), canal-hoppers (small open electric boats) in the summer, and canal bikes (pedalos) for the energetic.

The bridge to the Passenger Terminal

Bicycle

There are 750,000 people in Amsterdam, 600,000 bikes and 400 kilometres of cycling paths. There are lots of bicycle tours (p.110) and places to hire a bike (see below), but remember that cycling and sightseeing can be hard to do at the same time. Residents, you will notice very quickly, do not dawdle. But for getting out into the countryside or exploring outer zones of the city, a bike is unbeatable.

Do obey the rules – cyclists may look pretty casual in terms of their road use (riding insouciantly through red lights) but the police are getting hotter on fines. Helmets are not common (or indeed cycling clothing) but don't let that stop you choosing to wear one or putting one on your children.

Bike Rental Companies

DutchBike	020 683 33 69	www.dutchbikeamsterdam.nl
MacBike	020 620 09 85	www.macbike.nl
Mike's Bike Tours	020 622 79 70	www.mikesbikeamsterdam.com
Orangebike	020 528 99 88	www.orangebike.nl
Rent-a-Bike	020 625 50 29	www.bikes.nl
Star Bikes Rental	020 330 81 32	www.starbikesrental.com

Bus

There's an extensive network of buses, which is particularly important for areas trams don't reach, such as the suburbs and Amsterdam Noord, and 23 nightbus routes (for which you need a different strippenkart). Regional Connexxion buses service the countryside. For leisurely 'gable spotting' (p.59), hop on the 'Stop/Go', bus (formerly known as the opstapper) which trundles all the way from Oosterdock to the Stopera on Waterlooplein. Just stick out your arm, and it will stop (very Harry Potter), then tell the driver when you want to get off. It costs a €1 and the ticket is valid for an hour.

Ferry

It only takes about a minute to get to Amsterdam Noord on one of the free ferries, leaving regularly all day from De Ruyterkade behind Centraal Station. There are six routes in total going west to NDSM, straight across to Buiksloterweg and IJplein, and east to Java Island (which is charged at €1 a trip). Two routes run from Houthaven (to the west of Centraal Station) to NDSM and Distelweg in Amsterdam Noord. For more details, see www.gvb.nl.

There's also a high-speed jetfoil (run by regional operator Connexxion – see www.connexxion.nl for timetables and prices) that goes to IJmuiden. There are also water taxis available for rent (www.water-taxi.nl, 020 535 6363), and prices start at around €60 for the first half hour.

Metro

Amsterdam's metro is relatively modern and designed to connect outlying suburbs to the city, rather than transporting passengers around it. Despite this it can be extremely fast for particular journeys (Centraal Station to the Stopera, for example). Routes and timetables can be found on the website www.gvb.nl. It's controversial expansion (North-South line) is in the process of being built.

Rail

Trains are reliable and frequent in the Netherlands and reach areas not served directly by trams or buses. Fares are reasonable. The website www.ns.nl gives info in English on routes and tickets. Many trains are double deckers and you can often take your bike on them. You must buy (or stamp) a ticket before you board, and you need a special ticket for your bike as well. Ticket inspection is frequent and so are fines. Amsterdam has international rail links to Belgium, France and Germany.

Self-Drive

Cars in the Netherlands drive on the right hand side of the road. Unless otherwise marked, the speed limit is 50kph in the city, 80kph on other roads and 100/120kph on motorways. A car will be a nuisance in the centre of Amsterdam. Parking is problematic with approximately 100,000 (expensive) metered parking places on the streets and 10 multistorey carparks (including seven in the centre).

Meter hours are 09:00 to 24:00, Monday to Saturday, and 12:00 to 24:00 on Sundays. Parking is zoned and costs €4.40 an hour in the centre, less outside the centre. There is, however, a park and ride scheme at four locations, with free public transport by tram, train, metro, bus or bike into the city centre (see www.bereikbaaramsterdam.nl for more driving and parking information).

Hiring A Car

There is no shortage of places to hire a car, with international agencies well represented. See the table (right) or check

Autoverhuur in the Yellow Pages (Gouden Gids) to get local quotes. It is worth shopping around as prices vary quite a lot. In terms of models to hire, there is a complete range, from small city cars for urban driving to something more deluxe. Prices (at the small, neat end) start from around €30 to €35 a day and rise to €100 plus for a seven seater.

Car Rental Agencies

Adams Rent-a-Car	020 685 01 11	www.adamsrentacar.nl
Alamo	020 616 24 66	www.alamo.nl
Avis Car Rental	020 683 60 61	www.avis.nl
Budget	020 612 60 66	www.budget.nl
Europcar	020 683 21 23	www.europcar.nl
Hertz	020 612 24 41	www.hertz.nl
National	0800 6284 6625	www.nationalcar.nl

Taxi

There are designated areas for taxi stands (including Centraal Station, Rembrandtplein and Leidseplein, where there are always plenty waiting) and regulations about where they might stop. You can also hail one in the street (bear in mind there are several no-stopping zones) or book one over the phone (TCA 020 777 77 77).

Every taxi must have blue number plates, a price list visible from both inside and outside the taxi, and a taxi-driver's pass on the dashboard. If they have an exemption card – meaning they have passed an exam testing their city knowledge – they can use the tram and bus lanes. You are not legally obliged to take the first taxi in the queue (although if you don't, it will not be a popular action). Taxis are metered and most include sat-nav systems so you will be able to get to your destination, but local knowledge varies considerably. The maximum base price is €5.12 (for four or more passengers, €8.33), and the maximum price per kilometre is €1.94 (for four or more passengers, €2.23). A taxi from the airport to a central Amsterdam hotel is around €40 and from Centraal Station to Museumplein, around €13.

Tram

Amsterdam has 16 tramlines and 232 trams, which travel over 80 kilometres of track. Routes and timetables can be seen on the website www.gvb.nl, and you pay on the tram or stamp your strippenkart. Once stamped, your ticket can be used for up to one hour on other trams or alternative modes of transport.

Many trams start their journeys from Centraal Station. Unlike the bus and metro, trams travel through the main shopping streets. Recent expansion includes tram 26 to the eastern IJburg archipelago. Newer-style trams can accommodate wheelchairs and baby buggies. Trams stop around midnight, when night buses come into operation.

Walking

Amsterdam is a compact city and easy to navigate as a pedestrian, but watch out for the bikes and bollards, and absolutely no wandering into the fietspad (bicycle lane). At all times watch your step – this is dog poop city.

Clockwise from top left: Amsterdam RAI metro station, bike park by Centraal Station, Amsterdam's tram system

Places To Stay

From the grandest location on the Amstel to a cosy houseboat bobbing about in Jordaan, there's a wealth of places to stay.

Amsterdam has almost 350 hotels and 18,000 rooms, together with hostels, houseboats, private apartments and campsites that provide accommodation for every taste and budget. Room rates (which are dependent on hotel occupancy) fluctuate wildly, even in high season. You can often get a great rate on a Sunday, but some hotels have a three-night minimum stay. A 5% city tax may or may not be included in the price and breakfast is often extra. Amsterdam's hotels are mainly clustered around the the centre, the canals, the museum area and Vondelpark. The Dutch Hotel Classification system (www.hotelsterren.nl) awards stars on a points-based system according to services and facilities available. There are no extra points for staff charm or architectural loveliness.

The Amstel InterContinental tops the deluxe price league in Amsterdam at €595 to €4,000 a night, but there are four-star venues which deliberately don't want to be five star, because it

The Euro Sign

The euro sign is intended to give a rough idea of costs. These are based on prices in mid 2008 for a double room, and are subject to change.

€ – under €50
€€ – €50-€100
€€€ – €100-€200
€€€€ – €200-€300
€€€€€ – €300+

Victoria Hotel

deters business and conference bookers, and some utterly charming venues with fewer stars. In the centre, canal-side hotels are situated in (one or several) 17th and 18th century residences. Elegant, cosy, full of art and antiques, these can be wonderful places to stay. Rooms veer towards the snug rather than spacious. The Dylan Hotel has long been a benchmark for boutique hotels, but the last few years have seen more entrants into Amsterdam's hip list.

The latest include the five-star Amrâth housed in the historic Scheeepvarthuis (Shipping Office) and at the other end of the scale, Amsterdam's first budget designer hotel, the Qbic, which is located in the financial district (and development zone) of Amsterdam South. Two new design-conscious Schiphol options that opened in 2008 include the 55 cabin pod hotel Yotel (www.yotel.com) and the first CitizenM hotel (www.citizenm.com). Book accommodation online at www.booking.com or www.hotelres.nl or via the tourist office (for a small fee).

Ambassade Hotel

www.ambassade-hotel.nl

020 555 02 22

A haven of opulent elegance located in 10 17th century canal houses. Popular with literary types, many of the 59 rooms have original art from the CoBrA movement.

€€€

Map 6 B4 **1**

Amstel InterContinental

www.amsterdam.intercontinental.com

020 622 60 60

Amsterdam's grandest and most luxurious hotel has been a stately presence on the Amstel since 1867, with a pool, wonderful terraces and a renowned restaurant.

€€€€€

Map 10 D1 **2**

The Dylan

www.dylanamsterdam.com

020 530 20 10

Set in 17th century surroundings, and one of the world's first boutique hotels, the dramatic interior is matched by an equally striking courtyard for alfresco dining.

€€€€€

Map 9 A1 **3**

Sofitel The Grand Amsterdam
www.thegrand.nl
020 555 31 11
A former convent, Admiralty HQ and city hall, the feel is of a grand country house with rooms, suites and apartments, and a delightful terrace and garden for taking tea.
€€€€€
Map 6 D2

Grand Hotel Amrâth Amsterdam
www.amrathamsterdam.com
020 552 00 00
Amsterdam's latest five-star grand is in the refurbished Scheepvaarthuis. The dramatic interior is monumental in scale, with decorative features and 164 (huge) rooms.
€€€€€
Map 3 F3

Hotel Pulitzer
www.pulitzer.nl
020 523 52 35
Comprising 25 linked 17th and 18th century houses, Hotel Pulitzer has a peaceful, private garden, which is a popular wedding reception location.
€€€€
Map 5 F3

Hotel Roemer

www.hotelroemer.nl

020 589 08 00

One of a pair of boutique hotels in Oud Zuid, there are chic interiors and great outside spaces. The designer terrace and peaceful lawns are open to non-residents.

€€€

Map 11 D2 **7**

Lloyd Hotel & Cultural Embassy

www.lloydhotel.com

020 561 36 36

A renovated 1920s building with one to five-star accommodation in 117 rooms styled by leading Dutch designers. Definitely not your average designer hotel.

€€

Map 1 E2

Mövenpick Hotel Amsterdam

www.moevenpick-amsterdam.com

020 519 12 00

A top location in the eastern docklands with spacious, stylish, contemporary design and stunning views over the IJ – be amazed at the cruise ships next door.

€€€

Map 1 D2

NH Grand Hotel Krasnapolsky
www.nh-hotels.nl
020 554 91 11
Amsterdam's biggest city centre hotel is located on Dam Square. There is non-stop bustle, with extensive conference activity, and it's a top spot for shoppers to stay.
€€€
Map 6 C1 🎱

Qbic WTC Amsterdam
www.qbichotels.com
04 321 11 11
Cheap and chic in the financial district, rooms start at €39. Each 'cubi' includes a bed, bathroom elements, communication technology and adjustable mood lighting.
€
Map 1 D4

Seven One Seven
www.717hotel.nl
020 427 07 17
Sumptuous and elegant, this unique canal-side house has eight luxurious suites decorated with a comfortable mix of antiques and artworks.
€€€€€
Map 9 C3 🎱

Apartments

If you find hotels anonymous and would like more space and privacy, there are lots of studios and apartments to rent. Do bear in mind that many Amsterdam houses are tall and narrow, with precipitous staircases (and no elevator). Rental periods vary, but anything less than three nights is unlikely.

Apartments

86 sous	06 29 035956	www.86sous.nl
Apartel	020 320 06 00	www.apartel.nl
Captain's Place	020 419 81 19	www.meesvof.nl
City Mundo	020 470 57 05	www.citymundo.com
Frederic Rentabike	020 624 55 09	www.frederic.nl

Bed & Breakfasts

Bed and breakfasts in Amsterdam (logie en ontbijt or L&O) are not necessarily cheap, as the more stylish options cost the same as (or even more than) a hotel. Facilities range from the basic to luxurious with ensuite facilities and designer furnishings in Golden Age mansions. They can provide additional options in areas of the city not smothered in hotels. B&B portal www. bedandbreakfast.nl lists over 100, and you can find

Houseboats

For a very different and magical experience, it's possible to stay on a houseboat. Good sources include Frederic Rentabike or City Mundo (see table above), or www.houseboathotel.nl. Prices range from €25 to €68 per person per night.

more on cheap digs at www.citymundo.com and www.find-an amsterdambed-and-breakfast.nl.

Hostels

One of the cheapest options, if not the quietest, a bed in a six to eight person dorm in hostels like The Shelter is only €16 a night. StayOkay by Vondelpark is a great venue for families or those who would like to sleep. For reviews and helpful info, see www.hostelamsterdam.com and www.hostels-amsterdam.nl.

Hostels		
The Bulldog Hotel	020 627 16 12	www.bulldoghotel.com
Flying Pig Hostels	020 421 05 83	www.flyingpig.nl
The Shelter Jordaan	020 624 47 17	www.shelter.nl
Stayokay	020 639 10 35	www.stayokay.com

Campsites

The Dutch love camping, and there are several sites within easy reach of the city. A four-person tent at Zeeburg costs €5 plus €5 per person, but you can also rent cabins; a two-person cabin is €40. Transport to the city centre is straightforward.

Campsites		
Amsterdamse Bos	020 641 68 68	www.campingamsterdamsebos.nl
De Badhoeve	020 490 42 83	www.campingdebadhoeve.nl
Vliegenbos	020 636 88 55	www.vliegenbos.com
Zeeburg	020 694 44 30	www.campingzeeburg.nl

Exploring

Explore Amsterdam

Relaxed Amsterdam is a wanderer's delight. Meander on foot, cycle like the locals or hop on a tram or bus. It's all so easy to explore.

Amsterdam is an intimate and supremely accessible city that is perfect to explore both on foot or by that quintessentially Dutch form of transport – the bicycle. This chapter delves into each of Amsterdam's key districts with some top tips for every area. In the maps at the back, you can locate all the sights mentioned here. You will, of course, discover many more for yourself.

History, sex, education and religion are all well represented in the old part of the centre (Centrum, p.64), which starts just south and east of bustling Centraal Station. The medieval core, Red Light District, Nieuwmarkt, Dam Square and Koninklijk Paleis (Royal Palace) are in this area, with literary headquarters, Spui, a graceful respite in the middle of the shopping zone.

Looping round Centrum is the elegant girdle of grand canals (p.72) that gives Amsterdam its distinctive shape. Lined with magnificent 17th and 18th century gabled mansions, a leisurely wander up one of these canals, with their Golden Age gems, will provide some of the most vivid images of your visit.

When you are lost (and you will be), the towering spire of the Westerkerk is the landmark for the famous Anne Frank Huis. Once you cross over the Prinsengracht, the northern part of Jordaan is home to charming waterways and intriguing narrow streets stuffed with a myriad of galleries, cosy cafes and quirky shopping opportunities.

Lying south of the Canal Belt is the elegant Oud Zuid (p.80), with the museum district and Concertgebouw – one of the best concert halls in the world. The swankiest zone for designer-label shopping is on P.C. Hooftstraat, but you can also escape to the mile-long Albert Cuypstraatmarkt in the hip district, De Pijp. On this side of town, the gates leading into the romantic Vondelpark are very splendid indeed.

Opposite the Amstel, where the grand canals terminate, is the Oost (p.88). This is the old Jewish corner of the city, which continues out east along the wide leafy streets of the Plantage. The Joods Historisch Museum (Jewish Historical Museum) is a top stop, along with the Stadhuis (city hall) and Muziektheater combo known as the Stopera, and behind it, Waterlooplein Market and Rembrandthuis.

But Amsterdam does not just luxuriate in its past. Along the waterfront to the east, a more futuristic version of the city can be seen in the regenerating docklands, with startling architecture such as the swoopy-roofed Passenger Terminal Building and the Muziekgebouw, marking the start of Zeeburg (p.94). These join the experimental creations on Java and KNSM islands and Sporenburg and Borneo peninsulas. And the city isn't finished yet: in IJburg, a new archipelago of seven islands is a

Gable Spotting

The Canal Belt (p.72) is prime territory for gable spotting. Look out (and up) for step, spout, neck and bell gables decorating the front apex of roofs and cunningly placed vases or ornaments that cover some architectural irregularities.

At A Glance

Looking for a specific museum, gallery or park? This handy list will help you tick off all the important attractions.

Art Galleries

Beaches

Churches

Museums & Heritage Sites

Regulersgracht and Keizersgracht

Centrum

Amsterdam's lively centre is where the city was born. It's the area for shopping, socialising and history.

The city's most historic buildings can be found in the centre, which has both old and new sides. Dam Square, despite the Royal Palace (Koninklijk Paleis, p.66), is actually rather dull, although architecture fans should check out the iconic Beurs van Berlage on the (otherwise tacky) Damrak. The warren of canals and alleys making up the Red Light District (p.69) and its borders contain some terrific historical details, despite the sleazy surroundings, while the bars and cafes surrounding Nieuwmarkt in Amsterdam's little Chinatown, and in literary Spui with its many bookshops, are great places for a drink. Top cultural wanderings include Amsterdams Historisch Museum (p.65) and the charming Begijnhof (p.65). *For restaurants and bars in the area, see p.172. For shopping, see Markets p.150 and Malls & Department Stores p.152.*

Cohen Cleans Up

Mayor Job Cohen has started plans to clean up the city by reducing the number of windows in the Red Light District. In 2007, a third of the windows were bought back from their landlord and rented out free to fashion designers, instead of the famous women. Renewal of licences for sex clubs are also being declined – all in an attempt to cut the links between the sex industry and organised crime.

The Amsterdam Dungeon

020 530 85 30

Rokin 78   www.theamsterdamdungeon.nl

A fun and fact-filled experience incorporating live actors, special effects and a great rollercoaster ride, all of which escort you back to some gruesome chapters in Dutch history. Map 6 C3 ■

Amsterdams Historisch Museum

020 523 18 22

Kalverstraat 92   www.ahm.nl

Originally built as the city's orphanage, this wonderful museum, housed in a warren of 17th century buildings, does full justice to Amsterdam's fascinating history through art, artifacts and film. If you want to understand the city's watery origins and phenomenal growth, this is the place to go. Kids love it: you can ride a bicycle, drive a car and winch a horse out of the canal. The civic guards gallery is good practice for viewing *The Nightwatch* at the Rijksmuseum. Map 6 C3 ■

Begijnhof

020 622 19 18

Begijnensloot   www.begijnhofamsterdam.nl

A tranquil hideaway situated off one of the busiest streets in the city, these houses are located around a tranquil glade of grass, trees and flowers. It was originally occupied by the Beguines, an order of lay nuns founded in the 15th century (the last ones died in the 1970s). Number 34 is the oldest wooden house in the Netherlands. The Engelse Kerk, or English Church celebrated its 400th anniversary in February 2007 when Queen Elizabeth II joined Queen Beatrix for a tour. There are more hofjes (p.77) in Jordaan and the canal belt. Map 6 C4 ■

Beurs van Berlage
Damrak 277

020 530 41 41
www.beursvanberlage.nl

The former stock exchange, designed by Hendrick Berlage and completed in 1903, is an iconic landmark in Dutch 20th century architecture. It is used today as a concert hall and a venue for exhibitions. Map 3 C4 **4**

Hermitage Amsterdam
Nieuwe Herengracht 14

020 530 87 55
www.hermitage.nl

This is a satellite branch of the Hermitage Museum in St Petersburg. Amsterdam's relations with Russia actually date back 300 years and Czar Peter the Great spent time learning shipbuilding in the Netherlands. Each exhibition is jointly curated by St Petersburg and Amsterdam. The museum is located over three floors in the historic Amstelhof and has expansion plans. Map 7 A3 **5**

Holland Casino
Max Euweplein 62

020 521 11 11
www.hollandcasino.nl

Truth be told, it's not Vegas, but it's a chance to try your hand against a Dutch dealer (cards that is). Here's a hint… it's so un-Vegas that the drinks aren't free, but if you are a fan of *Casino Royale* then this is your best bet. Map 9 B4 **6**

Koninklijk Paleis
Dam Square

020 620 40 60
www.koninklijkhuis.nl

The Royal Palace on Dam Square was originally built as Amsterdam's City Hall (in 1648) but was converted into a Palace with Louis Napoleon's arrival in 1808. The large

Damrak

collection of empire-style furniture, chandeliers and clocks date from this period. The palace is still used for official functions by the Dutch Royal Family but is open to the public at other times. Guided tours for groups all year round, by appointment. Map 6 B2 **7**

De Nieuwe Kerk

Dam Square

020 638 69 09
www.nieuwekerk.nl

Adjacent to the Royal Palace on the Dam, the 14th century church is only 'new' in relation to the Oude Kerk, which predates it by more than a century. Located on Dam Square next to the Palace, the church is famous not only for its Gothic architecture but also its regular exhibitions. This is an extremely popular venue – the museum has more than half a million visitors every year. Its most famous inhabitant is iconic Dutch naval hero Admiral Michiel de Ruyter. Map 6 B1 **8**

Nieuwmarkt & De Waag
Near Gelderskade

Follow Zeedijk all the way from the Centraal Station end and you arrive in Nieuwmarkt, an open space filled with cafes, bars, Amsterdam's Chinatown and the hulking, multi-turreted presence of ex-weigh house De Waag (St Antoniespoort) – one of three gatehouses to the old city. Public executions were regular events and Rembrandt sketched dissections at the anatomical theatre. The building, once garnished with body parts, now houses a variety of enterprises including an atmospheric cafe. Steak rare, was it? Map 3 E4 9

Ons' Lieve Heer op Solder
020 624 66 04
Oudezijds Voorburgwal 40   www.museumamstelkring.nl

Also known as the Amstelkring Museum, this is an amazing combination of museum, house, secret church and chapel and a beautifully atmospheric trip through the art and design of the 1660s. It was built during the period when Dutch Catholics were no longer permitted to worship in public (although tolerated, in secret). The church has 150 seats and a large altar and services were held in the church until 1887. Map 3 D3 10

Oude Kerk
020 625 82 84
Oudekerksplein 23   www.oudekerk.nl

In the middle of the Red Light District is Amsterdam's oldest monument dating back to 1250. Partly destroyed by fire (1421 and 1452) and heavily looted during 'the Alteration' when Protestants took over from Catholics, it's a mix of gothic and renaissance architecture with later editions such as dinky boxed pews for the gentry. The superb 1724 Vater-Müller Organ features in John Irving's novel *Until I Find You*. There's still a Sunday service, but the building mostly serves as a venue for concerts and major exhibitions such as the annual World Press Photography Awards. Rembrandt's first wife Saskia is buried here. Map 3 D4 **11**

St Nicolaaskerk
020 624 87 49

Prins Hendrikkade 73

As soon you exit Centraal Station you will notice the towers and gilded cupola of this neo-Renaissance Catholic church. Located at the position where the Amstel flowed into the city, the church is well placed because St Nicholas is, among other things, the patron saint of seafarers. It is an impressive building, both inside and out, and was the first to be built in the city following the repeal of religious restriction and continues to be the main place of worship for the city's Catholics. Map 3 D2 **12**

Red Light District (De Wallen)
South-east of Damrak

Famous for its women in the windows, this is an area that (almost) everyone has to visit once. It is most evident between Oudezijds Achterburgwal canal in the east and Warmooesstraat in the west. But it's not all sex in the city. Zeedijk and Warmoesstraat have their share of historic bars and shops, the area is home to Oude Kerk (left), and the local name, De Wallen (the walls), comes from the defenses surrounding the oldest part of town. Only one no-no – don't photograph the women in windows. Map 3 D4 **13**

If you only do one thing in...
Centrum

Visit the Oude Kerk (p.68). Amsterdam's oldest building has an extraordinary atmosphere.

Best for...

Drinking: Spacious, light, grand café De Jaren (p.173) and its fabulous waterside terrace.

Eating: Go Dutch at Greetje (p.176), home to new Dutch cuisine and an old-world atmosphere.

Culture: The Amsterdams Historisch Museum (p.65) is anything but dull.

Relaxation: Get away from it all in the Begijnhof (p.65) – an oasis of calm in the shopping district.

Sightseeing: The historic centre and unusual church-in-the-attic museum, Ons' Lieve Heer op Solder (p.68).

Canal Belt & Jordaan

Amsterdam's canal district, lined with historic gabled mansions, is famous the world over, and packed with many places to explore.

Canals don't get grander than Amsterdam's girdle of Golden Age waterways stretching from the Brouwersgracht to the Leidsegracht, through the Golden Bend and all the way south to the Amstel. Lined by magnificent 17th and 18th century mansions, a separate district (the Jordaan) housed the workers that built them. Initially a home for artists, exiles, immigrants and smelly industry, Jordaan became a notorious slum.

Nothing could be more different now. Full of narrow tree-lined streets, charming canals, architectural idiosyncrasies and great cafes and restaurants, it's an exceptionally desirable neighbourhood occupied by a bohemian mixture of artists, yuppies, expats and hanging in there, a core of working-class residents. If you fancy a sing-a-long with the locals in a brown bar with carpets on the table, this is the district for you.

Jordaan's numerous art galleries are worth a browse (see p.74/6). Also, look out for notices announcing open atelier days ,when artists open their studios to the public. To check what's on where, www.akka.nl, www.mediamatic.nl and www. galleries.nl are essential arty references.

The Grand Canals

As well as the attractions listed in this section, some of the other buildings are also interesting for their external features, their history, or just the chance to see inside these beautiful canal houses. On Herengracht, see possibly the most beautiful house in Amsterdam, The Neufville House at No 475; admire the neck gable of the Theater Instituut at No 168; or see The Bartolotti House at No 170-172, which is a 17th century double house.

On Keizersgracht, No 123 is 'The House with Heads', after six burglars who were decapitated by a maid. She married the seventh. Museum Geelvinck Hinlopen Huis at No 633 has four recently restored rooms for viewing on weekends. At No 672, Museum van Loon is the most charming of the canal house museums. Or if you want to see inside a houseboat, opposite 296 Prinsengracht, there's the Houseboat Museum.
For restaurants and bars in the area, see p.184. For shopping, see Hotspots p.142-7 and Markets p.148 and p.150-1.

Anne Frank Huis
Prinsengracht 26, Canal Belt

020 556 71 00
www.annefrankhuis.nl

Anne Frank hid here for over two years during the second world war with her parents and sister, the Von Pels family and dentist Fritz Pfeffer, writing her famous diary. Walking through the museum's secret rooms and climbing the impossibly tiny stairs provoke a depth of feeling and silence among visitors. On 4 August 1944, the Gestapo raided the house and her father Otto was the only one to survive the camps. Map 5 E2 **14**

De Duif
Prinsengracht 756, Canal Belt (Grachtengordel)

020 520 00 70

Across from the Amstelkerk is this former Catholic church (aka The Dove), the first to be built after the French Government occupying the city declared there to be freedom of religion in Amsterdam following the Protestant Reformation. The organ in particular is breathtaking in size, as it reaches straight up to the high vaulted ceilings above. The Dove is a place of worship, and home to many cultural events. Map 10 A2 **15**

FOAM

020 551 6500

Keizersgracht 609, Canal Belt   www.foam.nl

This top photography museum is located in a converted canal house and holds international shows (Kate Moss, Weegee). It also shows both historical and contemporary images from Dutch archives to exhibitions from developing talent. A true cultural landmark. Map 9 E2 **16**

Gallery Vassie

020 489 40 42

Eerste Tuindwarsstraat 16, Jordaan   www.hughug.info

Originally known as the Hug Gallery, Gallery Vassie is owned and curated by Addie Vassie, formerly of the Victoria & Albert Museum in London. It represents internationally renowned artists such as Lee Miller, Antoni + Alison, Jason Oddy and Cornel Lucas. Map 5 D1 **17**

Huis Marseilles Museum for Photography

020 531 8989

Keizersgracht 401, Canal Belt   www.huismarseille.nl

Based in a 17th century canal house (and they've just bought the one next door), this is a top stop for photography buffs. There are new exhibitions every three months covering a broad range of international photographic genres. Map 9 B1 **18**

Clockwise from top left: Queen's Day on the canals, Binnen Vissersstraat, boat tour on Regulersgracht

Montevideo/Time Based Arts

020 623 71 01
www.montevideo.nl

Keizersgracht 264, Centrum

This gallery has been championing new technologies in the visual arts since 1978, with art installations encompassing both visual and sound-based formats. The institute is known for tirelessly supporting the most advanced and avant garde movements. There's a small charge for exhibitions. Take a look at the extensive website for more details. Map 5 F4 **19**

Museum Willet-Holthuysen

020 523 18 22
www.willetholthuysen.nl

Herengracht 605, Canal Belt

This furnished canal house is open daily to the public. Construction was completed in 1690 and it was a fashionable home to more than 20 families until the death of its last owners Abraham Willet (1825-1888) and his wife Louisa Holthuysen (1824-1895). On show are a vast array of paintings, ceramics, glassworks, silver, furniture and sculpture as well as a beautiful French-style garden. Map 6 F4 **20**

Noorderkerk

020 626 64 36

Noordermarkt 48, Jordaan

The Noorderkerk, the poor people's church (the Westerkerk was for the posh), was completed in 1623 and holds regular Dutch Reformed Church services. It's also a popular venue for classical concerts. The Noordermarkt, the square in front of it, has some notable cafes (wondrous apple cake at Winkel) and restaurants (Bordewijk) and holds popular markets on Mondays (antiques and clothes) and Saturdays (biological farmers' market). Map 2 D3 **21**

Pianola Museum

020 627 9624
Westerstraat 106, Jordaan
www.pianola.nl

This small museum is an enchanting place to visit, with regular concerts and a real 'ghost in the machine' feel when you watch the piano keys move. Long-dead pianists and composers come back to life in the room with you, playing the piano just as when they recorded the music 70 years ago. Map 2 D4 22

Tassenmuseum Hendrijke

020 524 6452
Herengracht 573, Canal Belt
www.tassenmuseum.nl

A whole museum devoted to handbags? Fabulous! Housed in an elegant 17th century mansion with a cafe overlooking the beautiful garden, there are 3,500 objects in the collection. The shop sells a wide selection of Dutch and internationally designed handbags together with loads of other gift ideas. Map 9 B1 23

Westerkerk

020 624 77 66
Westermarkt, Canal Belt

The central point of worship for Amsterdam's Dutch Reformed community, this church was the golden flagship for the rich burghers of the city in the 17th century. Highlights are the organ, which is covered in decorative panels, and the bell tower with over 160 steep steps. Rembrandt van Rijn is buried here in an unmarked grave. Map 5 E2 24

Hofjes

Hofjes are hidden courtyards with almshouses built around them, which provided sheltered housing to elderly women. The most famous is Begijnhof (p.65).

If you only do one thing in...
Canal Belt & Jordaan

Take a leisurely stroll along a canal – take your pick, and try The Grand Canals for starters (p.72) for some gablespotting (p.59).

Best for...
Drinking: One (or several) of Jordaan's brown bars such as Café Chris (p.167).

Eating: Head to canal-side cafe Buffet van Odette (p.185) for a scrumptious breakfast or lunch.

Shopping: Browse all day in the quirky Negen Straatjes (p.146) and Leidsestraat (p.154).

Sightseeing: The Anne Frank Huis (p.73) is justifiably renowned.

Culture: Experience Golden Age glory inside the Museum Willet-Holthuysen (p.76).

Oud Zuid & De Pijp

For culture, classical music, the city's most cherished park and some swanky shops and cafes, head south.

South of the Canal Belt is Oud Zuid, (or Old South), home to some of the city's swankiest addresses. Known as the culture zone, it contains the Museum Quarter, where, surrounding the open spaces of Museumplein are the Rijksmuseum, the Van Gogh Museum and the world-famous Concertgebouw concert halls (see p.218).

Label shoppers will find relief on Cornelis Schuytstraat or on P.C. Hoofstraat – the land of Bulgari, Cartier and Armani. But on a sunny day, what could be nicer than a picnic? Stock up at the mile-long Albert Cuypstraat Markt (p.148) in De Pijp and stretch out in Vondelpark – a delight for kids and grown-ups. Look out for the flocks of parakeets squawking in the trees.

For art and antiques, Nieuwe Spiegelstraat and Spiegelgracht (p.147) leading up to the Rijksmuseum are the smart antiques streets. Fine art, tribal art, scientific instruments, you'll find it all here.

Stiletto Sprint

Strap on your heels (nine centimetres minimum) for the *Glamour* Magazine Stiletto Run, which clacks down P.C. Hooftstraat every spring. The winner gets €10,000 to spend on clothes and accessories.

De Pijp

It's hip, it's hot, and it's a fantastic place to play. De Pijp is the hideaway of artists, musicians and students and has a real multicultural concentration. Painters like Mondriaan made De Pijp their home and many of the streets are named after artists. The Heineken Brewery once dominated the area, but it is now a museum. The cafes and restaurants are popular draws but number one is Albert Cuypstraat Markt (p.148). With 300 stalls, it sells pretty much everything, but is particularly known for its fish, and its produce turns up at the myriad of exotic eateries.

*For **restaurants and bars** in the area, see p.196. For **shopping**, Beethovenstraat p.142 and P. C. Hooftstraat p.147.*

De Appel
Nieuwe Spiegelstraat 10, Oud Zuid

020 622 52 15
www.deappel.nl

A contemporary art centre with exhibitions and an international curatorial training programme. Many artists shown in the gallery are recently discovered international finds. It celebrated its 30th anniversary in 2005, and shows video and paintings among a huge number of other mediums. Map 9 D2

Galerie Delaive
Spiegelgracht 23, Oud Zuid

020 625 90 87
www.delaive.com

This thriving modern and contemporary art gallery, run by Nico Delaive for more than 25 years, is just up the road from the Reflex and is chock-a-block full of fantastic pieces. Showing artists such as Appel, Christo, Lichtenstein and Andy

Warhol alongside Degas and Chagall, the gallery is only one of three of its kind in the country to display such high level international artwork. Map 9 D4 🎴

Galerie Lieve Hemel
020 623 00 60
Nieuwe Spiegelstraat 3, Oud Zuid   www.lievehemel.nl
Conveniently located in the Spiegelhof arcade, this gallery, which has been run by Koen Nieuwendijk since 1968, focuses on contemporary Dutch realism and silver. Shows change at least five times a year, and the gallery window is a wonderful place to observe the maze of antiquities and art on display. Map 9 D2 🎴

Heineken Experience Museum
020 523 96 66
Stadhouderskade 78, Oud Zuid www.heinekenexperience.com
Based in the old Heineken brewery, this gives an insight into the company's prestigious history. The tour follows the route of a bottle of the amber liquid as it takes the necessary steps to move from barley to beer. The experience lasts approximately one hour. The €10 charge can seem a bit steep, but you do get a couple of 'top ups' and can keep your souvenir glass. Be aware that the museum gets extremely crowded in summer. Map 12 C1 🎴

Jaski Art Gallery
020 620 39 39
Nieuwe Spiegelstraat 29, Oud Zuid   www.jaski.nl
A fine and friendly gallery specialising in the CoBrA movement which attracts many American visitors due to the large CoBrA museum in Florida. Alongside artists

such as Karel Appel, Jaski also exhibits works by renowned modern artists such as Rob Scholle, Andy Warhol and Herman Brood. Map 9 D3 **29**

Platform21
020 301 8000

Prinses Irenestraat 19, Buitenveldert   www.platform21.com

Platform21 is a creative hothouse bringing together contemporary art, fashion, issues and design in a developing space in Zuidas. It is currently housed in a beautiful chapel, but a new 5,000 square metre home is in the planning stages. Superhip Restaurant AS is on ground floor. Map 1 D4

Reflex Modern Art Gallery/
New Art Gallery
020 627 28 32

Weteringschans 79a, Oud Zuid   www.reflex-art.nl

This is a modern and contemporary art gallery which mainly features photography and video installations. Conveniently located directly across the canal from the Rijksmuseum, there are six to eight different shows a year, featuring either a solo artist or group. Its sister, Reflex New Art Gallery is across the road; both are closed on Sundays and Mondays. Map 9 D4 **31**

Rijksmuseum
020 674 70 47

Jan Luijkenstraat 1, Oud Zuid   www.rijksmuseum.nl

Renovations continue until 2010, but highlights are on show in The Philips Wing with Delftware, silver and paintings by Dutch masters such as Jan Steen, Vermeer and of course, Rembrandt. This is the home of *The Nightwatch*, which apparently has more than 200 secrets hidden within it. Is it a simple depiction of the city's prominent citizens (who each paid to appear in it), or the J'accuse of its day, telling the story of a murder? Map 12 A1 🟦

Sarphatipark
Nr Albert Cuypstraat, De Pijp

Located in the heart of De Pijp just two minutes from the market, this is a green space in a crowded space and it's extremely well used by the local population. The park is named after urban planner and philanthropist Samuel Sarphati (also involved in the nearby Amstel Hotel). You'll find his statue in the park. Though great in the daytime, it is deserted at night. Deservedly or not, it doesn't have a great reputation for safety. Map 12 F2 🟦

Van Gogh Museum
Paulus Potterstraat 7, Oud Zuid

020 570 52 00
www.vangoghmuseum.nl

This museum contains the largest collection of art by Vincent Van Gogh in the world: 200 paintings, 437 drawings and 31 prints. It also allows visitors to put the artist into context alongside his contemporaries, through work displayed from other artists of his time. Friday nights find the museum filled with armchairs, video screens, DJs, and a bar – it stays open till 22:00 as a venue for locals to meet. There are outstanding audio tours. Map 11 F3 🟦

Why De Pijp?
It is so-named because the narrow streets are shaped like the stem of a pipe, or perhaps because of the Pipe gas company, which used to supply the neighbourhood.

Oudebrugsteeg

Vondelpark

020 678 16 78

1e Constantijn Huygensstraat, Oud Zuid   www.vondelpark.nl

This large park is cherished by the whole city, with 45 hectares of greenery in which to wander, skate or loll about by the lakes. It attracts 10 million visitors each year and is rarely quiet – this is a place to people-watch rather than escape from it all. There are six children's play areas, skate rentals and lots of cafes. The summer brings free concerts and performances at the open-air theatre, while Cafe Vertigo above the Filmmuseum (www.filmmuseum.nl) is a grand spot for an evening drink. Or try one of the city's great hideaway cafes, Het Blauwe Theehuis (p.198). Map 11 C3 **35**

If you only do one thing in...

Oud Zuid & De Pijp

Join the dog walkers for an early breakfast or enjoy an evening cocktail at Blauwe Thee Huis (p.198).

Best for...

Eating: Time for tea? Don't miss the fabulously kitsch De Taart van m'n Tante (p.197).

Drinking: Cocktails at Ciel Bleu (p.200) on the 23rd floor of the Okura Hotel are full of wow factor.

Families: Smaller explorers have six playgrounds to choose from in the Vondelpark (p.85).

Culture: See Van Gogh's *Sunflowers* (p.84) and Rembrandt's *Nightwatch* (p.83) or just take a stroll around the Museum Quarter. Unmissable.

Shopping: Shoe Baloo (p.157) is a top spot on exclusive PC Hooftstraat (p.147).

Oost, Plantage & Jodenbuurt

This is an elegant part of the city, with poignant reminders of the past, as well as the excellent Artis Zoo.

Amsterdam's religious tolerance attracted Jews facing persecution in other countries from the 16th century. Many settled in Waterlooplein, with its famous market (p.151) and the Stopera, home to the Netherlands Opera and National Ballet. Joods Historisch Museum (p.90), arrange walks through the local neighbourhood, which was, prior to the second world war, Amsterdam's bustling Jewish quarter.

Pop inside the Stadhius, in Stopera, to learn about Amsterdam's water levels. Measured by a fixed point, the Normaal Amsterdams Peil (NAP) is based on the average level of the IJ in the 17th century, and is the basis for altitude measurements in Western Europe.

The leafy streets of the Plantage include Artis Zoo and Hortus Botanicus garden, and moving further east, the Oosterpark and KIT Tropenmuseum with renowned cultural exhibitions throughout the year. For a market, try the multi-culti Dapperstraat (p.149), one of Amsterdam's cheapest.

This area is also home to the city's most photographed bridge, the Skinny Bridge (Magere Brug), despite it not actually being that original, or very skinny. It was built by two sisters (the Magers) who lived on opposite sides of the Amstel, but wanted to see more of each other.

For restaurants and bars in the area, see p.204. For shopping, see Dapperstraat Markt p.149.

ARCAM

020 620 4878
www.arcam.nl

Prins Hendrikkade 600

The Architectuurcentrum is the top source for anything related to contemporary architecture. It has online guides to Amsterdam's newest constructions, links to architectural excursions, tour guides, exhibitions and information onsite. The amazing three-storey sculptural office was designed by Rene van Zuuk. It also offers around five exhibitions each year about architecture and urban development. Map 4 C3 36

Artis Zoo

020 523 34 00
www.amsterdamzoo.nl

Plantage Kerklaan 38-40, Plantage

A hugely popular institution, the oldest zoo in the Netherlands had its beginnings over 150 years ago. Get face to face with 700 species of fish, birds, mammals, insects and amphibians; the zoo's impressive aquarium even brings the secret life of Amsterdam's canals to the surface. Onsite (and included in the entry ticket) are the Planetarium, Geological Museum, Aquarium and Zoological Museum. Guided tours are available in English on Sundays at 11:00. Open every day of the year, from 09:00 to 17:00. During the summer Artis closes at 18:00. Torchlit tours during Museum Night. Map 4 F4 37

The Artis Express

During the summer season a special canal boat collects visitors from Amsterdam's Centraal Station and takes them to Artis Zoo. For more information call 020 530 10 90 or visit www.lovers.nl.

Frankendael

Linnaeusstraat 89, Watergraafsmeer   www.park-frankendael.nl

Originally the country manor of a wealthy 17th century Amsterdammer, the Frankendael ornamental park, covering seven hectares, is open to the public and provides a magnificent location for sunbathing, strolling and enjoying the sculptures on view. One section of the park has been developed into a botanical garden containing hundreds of varieties of plants and trees. Frankendael, just off of the Middenweg, is the only remaining (and preserved) country house in the city. Map 1 F2

Hortus Botanicus   020 625 90 21

Plantage Middenlaan 2a, Plantage   www.dehortus.nl

Part of the University of Amsterdam, the Hortus Botanicus is one of the world's oldest botanic gardens, containing almost 4,000 distinct species of plants growing both in greenhouse and garden settings. Stepping through the 300 year-old gates is surprisingly soothing. There's a fantastic medicinal herb garden, and the great Cafe De Oranjerie (p.167). Map 7 C2 38

Joods Historisch Museum   020 531 03 10

Nieuwe Amstelstraat 1, Centrum   www.jhm.nl

In the 1600s the city's Jewish community, which included philosophers such as Spinoza, was one of the most important in Europe. Based near the Portuguese Synagogue, the Jewish Historical Museum, is situated within a complex of several buildings, including the New and Great Synagogues, collects objects and works of art associated with the religion, culture and history of the Jews in the Netherlands and its colonies. It has an excellent children's wing. Map 7 B2 **39**

KIT Tropenmuseum

020 568 82 15

Linnaeusstraat 2, Oost   www.tropenmuseum.nl

You can never get bored at the KIT Tropenmuseum (the museum of the Royal Tropical Institute) with its massive collection of cultural anthropology – it's the largest museum of its kind in the Netherlands. There are eight permanent exhibitions and an extensive range of temporary presentations, through which visitors can experience different cultures and living conditions of the world's indigenous civilisations. It is an excellent venue for a wide range of culturally diverse world music, dance, debates, lectures and films. Map 1 F3

Rembrandthuis

020 520 04 00

Jodenbreestraat 4, Plantage   www.rembrandthuis.nl

Opened in 1999, this is an excellent window into the life and times of the artist and inveterate collector Rembrandt van Rijn. Entering his studio is an exquisite treat for any art lover, while next-door craftsmen demonstrate the etching techniques the master was renowned for. The museum has 260 of the 290 etchings Rembrandt produced, along with many items from his enormous collection. Map 6 F2 **40**

Free Concerts

On Tuesday lunchtimes, the Netherlands Opera performs at the Stopera. On Wednesdays, catch a free concert at the world-renowned Concertgebouw (p.218).

If you only do one thing in...
Oost, Plantage & Jodenbuurt

The Rembrandthuis (p.91) is a treat for any art lover, where you can sit at his easel.

Best for...

Drinking: The archetypal 'brown cafe', Elsa's (p.205) is a great local hangout.

Families: Say hello to Yindi the baby elephant. Artis Zoo (p.88) is great.

Shopping: Hunt for bargains at Dapperstraat, the 'best market in the Netherlands'. (p.149).

Culture: Check out performances from the Nederlands Opera (p.219).

Also In The Area: The Verzetsmuseum (www.verzetmuseum.org) provides a fascinating insight into Amsterdam's occupation by the Nazis and how it affected people's daily lives.

The Waterfront & Zeeburg

Along the waterfront is where the Amsterdam of the future is taking shape. There's great views, amazing architecture, and it's not finished yet.

Behind Centraal Station lies the IJ and a very different Amsterdam. To the west is the busy port, across the water is Amsterdam Noord, the city's most populous but least glamorous district, and to the east, starting from the stunning music venue Muziekgebouw aan 't IJ, the region of Zeeburg comprising Oostelijk Havengebied, the Indischebuurt and the new islands of IJburg.

Hire a bike (p.42) to zoom around the eastern docklands and Java Island (funky bridges and new canals), KNSM Island (1990s experimental housing) and the Borneo/Sporenbug peninsulas (red swoopy bridges). The area is awash with maritime landmarks, museums and some stunning modern architecture.

*For **restaurants and bars** in the area, see p.208.*

Blijburg aan Zee

Bert Haanstrakade 2004, Zeeburg

020 416 03 30
www.blijburg.nl

Part of the IJburg scene since its inception, Blijburg is both a beach and party place, and it's only a 15 minute tram ride from Centraal Station. Free entrance and a chilled out free-thinking crowd make Blijburg one of the best party places in Amsterdam's summer season. For those who know where to go, food, drinks, parties and fun are all readily available here. Don't forget your bucket and spade. Map 1 F1

NEMO
Oosterdok 2, Zeeburg

0900 919 1100
www.e-nemo.nl

The giant green building behind Amsterdam Centraal Station designed by Renzo Piano, is the biggest science centre in the Netherlands. The exhibits are designed to be interactive and spark a creative interest in the subject. Open since 1998, there are lots of hand-on exhibits popular with children from 6 to 16, but grown-ups will definitely enjoy it too. Pirate fans will love climbing aboard the replica VOC ship moored outside (it's normal berth is at the Scheepvartmuseum which is currently being renovated). Map 4 C2 41

NEMO Beach (BovenNEMO)
Oosterdok 2, Zeeburg

020 531 32 33
www.e-nemo.nl

Amsterdam's most central beach is located on the top of the sloping roof of NEMO science centre (above). You can grab a lounge chair or a beanbag, a few troughs of water and some food from the pretty steeply priced cafe, and enjoy the fantastic views out over the city. Map 4 C2 41

NDSM/Kinetisch Noord
NDSM-werf, Amsterdam Noord

020 3305480
www.ndsm.nl

With the decline of the shipbuilding industry in the 1970s, the huge empty shipyards and warehouses of NDSM, across in Amsterdam Noord, attracted squatters and artists in search of cheap space. Today it is one of Amsterdam's most creative zones operated by an umbrella organisation called Kinetisch Noord. There are markets, a skatepark, festivals such as Robodock and regular art events. Map 1 C1

Stedelijk Museum CS
020 573 29 11
Oosterdokskade 5, www.stedelijk.nl

While its permanent home in the Museum Quarter is under construction, the Stedelijk, one of Europe's most important venues for modern and contemporary art, has found a temporary home in the former Post CS building near Centraal Station. The tower block location has proved popular, not least because of Club 11 (p.181), the cafe, club and restaurant on the 11th floor with its stunning views. Map 4 A1 [43]

Amsterdam Plage
06 46 016005
Westerdokseiland www.amsterdamplage.nl

The Amsterdam Plage is a man-made beach, lying next to the Silodam industrial complex, behind Centraal Station. In addition to the incredibly unique location, there is a tasty cafe on site serving snacks, lunch and dinner. Take Tram 3 or Bus 48 to the Zoutkeetsgracht stop, then it's only a five minute walk to the beach. Swimming off the beach in Het IJ is not advised, but there is a pool. Map 1 C2

Local Knowledge

The next best thing to having cool, connected friends in Amsterdam is hiring a few. To arrange tours, sights, dinners, drinking or clubbing with local companions, check out www.like-a-local.com.

NEMO

If you only do one thing in...
The Waterfront & Zeeburg

Ride the ferry across the IJ and back. It only takes two minutes, and the trip is free.

Best for...

Drinking: Enjoy the fab views from the waterside Star Ferry cafe (p.209). Could this be Sydney?

Eating: Visit the stunning contemporary Star Ferry cafe (p.209) with its urban cool atmosphere and incredible views in every direction.

Outdoor: Lounge on the roof of NEMO (p.95) with great views out of the city.

Sightseeing: After enjoying lunch, take an eastern docklands bike tour to burn some calories (p.94).

Culture: Enjoy a concert at the beautiful Muziekgebouw aan 't IJ (p.209).

Further Out

Drag yourself away from Amsterdam for a few hours. Castles, windmills, bulb fields, quiet villages, historic towns and miles of windy beach all await.

The fast and efficient Dutch public transport system puts most of the Netherlands within a few hours reach of Amsterdam. Where trains (www.ns.nl) don't go, buses cover, and complete routes can be planned on the public transport information site (www.9292ov.nl), or with the help of the tourist information offices (VVV), see p.22, who can print itineraries and who run many excursions. If you are allergic to organised tours – and they can be a bit heavy on cheese and clogs – directions from Amsterdam are listed on most attractions' websites with, if you're driving, excellent signposting on the roads.

If you want to get really Dutch, and let's face it, fairly kitsch, how about the Clara Maria Cheese Farm and Clog Factory (Bovenkerkerweg 106, 0297 582 279) for a fun family day out in Amstelveen, just south of Amsterdam? Cheesy activities are laid on for tourists in the spring and summer at Alkmaar with its Friday morning cheese market, and in Gouda and Edam where, despite these towns having many other attractions, it is difficult to avoid the yellow stuff. The local tourist offices can provide details of walking tours and guides to the sights.

Not Van Gogh'd out yet? Head for the beautiful Kroller-Muller Museum and Sculpture Park (www.kmm.nl), where

Keukenhof

there are 300 more works by Van Gogh. You can also whiz about the Hoge Veluwe National Park (www.hogeveluwe.nl) on a free white bicycle. Utrecht (p.104), Delft (one hour) and Leiden (30 minutes) are all historic towns easily accessible from Amsterdam and well worth a visit.

The brilliant colours of the bulb fields in bloom attract tourists from all over the world, who head for South Holland in the spring. The season runs from late March to the beginning of May with different flowers (tulips, daffodils, hyacinths and narcissi) in bloom at different times. The Bollenstreek Route (bulb district route) takes in many small villages as well as Leiden, Noordwijk, Haarlem (p.108), Hillegom and the floral headquarters, Lisse, with the famed Keukenhof Gardens (p.102).

Another treat for floral fiends is the Aalsmeer flower auction (www.aalsmeer.nl), but it's an early start – trading opens at 06:00. It's the biggest in the world and several halls are in auction action at the same time. Visitors view the scene from catwalks suspended above the enormous trading halls and prices are dictated by the 'Dutch Auction' system in which prices go down, not up. A 'clock' on the wall shows the price descending until a dealer buzzes to buy at that price. The auction can be reached with the 172 bus that stops outside the American Hotel in the Leidseplein.

Keukenhof

Keukenhof (0252 465 555, www.keukenhof.nl) is the largest flowering gardens in the world, well earning their title 'The Garden of Europe', with a 17 acre park and greenhouse complex. Nearly seven million tulip bulbs are planted here and more exotic blooms grown under glass. Easy to get to by bus (the Keukenhof Express, which goes from Leiden, Haarlem (p.108) and Schiphol Airport); car (A4 to Leiden then N207 for Lisse); or to escape the crowds, by bicycle. On a two-wheeled tour (p.110) around the bulb-growing region you'll really appreciate the subtle scents and amazing colours close up, as if you were cycling through a painting by Van Gogh.

Zandaam & Zaanse Schans

There are a handful of windmills left in Amsterdam itself but a very accessible half-an-hour away is Zaanse Schans (www. zaanseschans.nl), a restored hamlet with characteristic green and white houses and little bridges, working windmills, cheese

Windmills at Zaanse Schans

farm (kaasboerderij), clog maker (Klompenmakerij), a couple of interesting museums (clocks and regional history) and the very first Albert Heijn. Sounds super-touristy? Well it is, but the windmills (www.zaansemolen.nl) are great. De Kat makes paint, De Zoeker pounds nuts and seeds into oil, and De Huisman delicious mustard. Climb the ladders to the top and sense the power of an industrial machine as the sails thunder past.

In Zandaam itself, the Czar Peter House is a reminder of an illustrious visitor (Peter the Great of Russia) who came to the Netherlands to learn shipbuilding. To get to Zaanse Schans, take the train to Koog-Zaandijk and follow the signs, or take the Connexxion bus 91 (both train and bus leave from Amsterdam Centraal Station). The pumping mills at Kinderdijk (www.kinderdijk.nl) under sail are a magnificent sight, and because there are 19 packed together in a small area (a

gang), there's a real sense of the 18th century landscape when thousands were whirling away. A bit of a trek from Amsterdam but worth combining with a visit to Rotterdam (p.108) – you have to get the train there anyway, and there's a nice boat trip from Rotterdam harbour to the mills, which is extremely popular. You can come home from the mills with some delicious mustard or vibrant-coloured authentic Dutch paint...the perfect souvenir from your time in Holland.

Utrecht

There are over 400 castles in the Netherlands, and Utrecht, just half an hour from Amsterdam, has several of the best, see www.utrechtsekastelen.nl. Muiderslot (www.muiderslot. nl) was built for Floris V in 1280. Hugely atmospheric with a moat, bullet holes in the thick walls, a jousting simulation game and elegant furnishings from when poet PC Hooft lived and lavishly entertained here, kids and grown-ups love it. Take bus 136 from Amstel Station.

Kasteel de Haar (www.kasteeldehaar.nl) certainly looks like an enchanted castle but many of the renovations are relatively recent. Take bus 127 from Utrecht. For a romantic stay in historic surroundings check out www.weekendhotel.nl for a kasteel hotel.

Seaside & Islands

Evidence of the Netherlands' nautical past can be seen in towns like Hoorn and Enkhuizen where the open-air Zuiderzeemuseum (www.zuiderzeemuseum.nl) is a top stop. Former fishing villages close to Amsterdam are an essential

Clockwise from top left: Sunset over the North Sea, Zandvoort Beach, flower fields near Keukenhof

element of folkloric tours in North Holland and in just one day you can easily do Marken (the least tacky), Voldendam (buy smoked eel), the scenic boat trip between them (the Marken Express), and squeeze in a visit to pretty Edam and Monnickendam as well (see p.100). Bus route 110 from Centraal Station connects all the villages. This is a great trip with a bicycle. Visit Broek-in-Waterland en route (the bus stops there too). It's a rich village with some interesting history and gardens and a nice lake to have a picnic by. You can hire canoes and boats here for a Waterland tour (see p.124).

The Netherlands' coastline attracts a wide variety of wildlife and is rich in vegetation. The Noord Holland Dune Reserve, which runs from Wijk aan Zee (p.123) – the widest beach on the Dutch coastline – to Bergen aan Zee is a popular route for walkers, cyclists and families, particularly since the inception of the children's kabouter (gnome) route, on which children hunt for gnomes while learning about the natural world.

There are some 40 resorts along the west and north coasts and popular seaside destinations for Amsterdammers include Castricum, resorty Zandvoort (p.123) – ultra accessible by train, hip Bloemendaal aan Zee (p.123) – bus from Haarlem, and the trio of Egmond villages.

Waddenlopen

You can walk across the tidal flats (wadden) from island to island in a guided tour – three hours plus – and get the uncanny sensation of standing in the middle of the sea. Contact the local tourist offices (www.noord-holland.com).

More suited for a weekend trip are the Wadden Islands (www.waddeneilanden.nl) that stretch across the north of the country, reached by ferry from Den Helder, Harlingen, Holwerd and Lauwersoog. Texel is the biggest, with six museums including a maritime museum (www.texelsmaritiem.nl) and seal sanctuary (www.ecomare.nl) but everyone has their favourite island. Terschelling is particularly famous for the annual Oerol Festival (www.oerol.nl) of theatre and music.

Den Haag (The Hague)

The seat of government, the home of foreign embassies and consulates and with an outpost for every major peace organisation in the world including the International Court of Justice, Den Haag has a much more stately feel than Amsterdam, and indeed it's where Queen Beatrix and Crown Prince Willem Alexander live and work. But it is also a very green city with many parks, attractive architecture and wide boulevards and the added bonus of a seaside resort, Scheveningen, on its perimeters.

There are copious monuments and museums celebrating the pride of the nation. The 'must sees' include the Anton Philips Concert Hall on Spuiplein; the beautiful Mauritshuis Museum (Korte Vijverberg 8, 070 302 34 56), which is home to a wonderful collection of paintings by the likes of Rembrandt, Hobbema, Rubens, and Vermeer, including his *Girl with a Pearl Earring*; and the utterly different, but fun M.C. Escher Museum (Lange Voorhout 74, 070 427 77 30), which is an absolutely riveting look at the revered Dutch graphic artist and his work.

Rotterdam

Where Amsterdam is cuddly and relaxed, Rotterdam (70 minutes by train) is hard-edged steel and glass – renowned for its futuristic skyline, innovative architecture (it was bombed heavily in the second world war) and businesslike ethics. A trip round the port (until recently the largest in the world) is fascinating, and check out museums like the Boijmans van Beuningen (www.boijmans.rotterdam.nl) with Old Masters and contemporary art, or zoom up 185 metres of the Euromast Space Tower (www.euromast.nl). The oldest statue in the Netherlands stands in front of St Laurenskerk on Grotekerkplein.

The statue is of scholar, philosopher, and Rotterdam native Desiderius Erasmus (1469-1536). Download a walking tour of landmarks like the cube buildings at www.rotterdam.info. In July, the North Sea Jazz Festival (www.northseajazz.nl) comes to town at the Ahoy.

Westergasfabriek

Although west Amsterdam doesn't have a lot to see, one place worth exploring is Westergasfabriek (020 586 07 10, www.westergasfabriek.nl) opposite Haarlemmerweg. This redeveloped industrial site is now home to creative, artistic and cultural events. There are bars, restaurants, a cinema and theatre, together with artists' studios and a skate park.

Haarlem

Just 15 minutes by train away, Haarlem is a quaint town that has a serenity quite different to Amsterdam. It is a wonderful place for strolling and discovering its

Canal in Amstelveenweg

17th and 18th century architecture, excellent art galleries and museums. The Grote Market is a great place to start your exploration. Must-sees include the imposing gothic church (Grote Kerk St Bavo's) and its enormous (30 metre tall) Müller organ that was played by Handel and Mozart in their time. The Teylers Museum (www.teylersmuseum.nl, 023 531 90 10) is the oldest museum in the Netherlands with a fascinating range of collections from fossils to scientific instruments as well as drawings by Michelangelo and Raphael.

Another star attraction is the Frans Hals Museum (www.franshalmuseum.nl, 023 511 57 75) with an impressive collection of Dutch Masters. For those looking to stay current rather than wallow in the past, Haarlem is a very popular destination for shopping and eating out: the variety of restaurants, cafes and terraces belies the small size of the town.

Tours & Sightseeing

Whether by bike, boat, bus or on foot, – there are lots of ways to see the city. If you're short of time or want some local knowledge, take a tour.

Bicycle Tours

Dutch cycle routes are well signposted so exploring solo shouldn't be a problem, but it's also fun to travel in a pack with a knowledgeable guide to explore the city and Dutch countryside. Hop on a bike and you can be cycling along a dijk with the wind in your hair, just moments after leaving the centre.

Cycletours Holland   020 521 84 90
Buiksloterweg 7A, Zeeburg   www.cycletours.com
These countrywide tours last several days, and combine sailing and cycling. The company combines a wide range of Dutch scenes which are all interesting treats for tourists. Evenings are spent on the company's sailing boat. Map 1 D1

Mike's Bike Tours   020 622 79 70
Kerkstratt 134, Centrum   www.mikesbikeamsterdam.com
Fantastic four-hour tours with friendly and knowledgeable guides giving the lowdown on the city centre then out to the countryside to visit a cheese farm and a clog making display. They also have a bike and boat tour, which lasts approximately five hours. Map 9 D3 59

Orange Bike Rentals and Tours

020 528 99 90

Singel 233, Centrum   www.orangebike.nl

Orange offers a wide variety of daily excursions including beach, culinary, historical city, gay areas and architectural heritage. In the spring, whiz off to see the tulips in the bulb-growing areas. Map 6 A2 60

Yellow Bike Tours

020 620 69 40

Nieuwezijds Kolk 29, Centrum   www.yellowbike.nl

Amsterdam's original bike tour company, and its most conspicuous, offers three-hour city tours and six-hour countryside tours with excellent guides. Tours are limited to 12 people, and run from April to November. Map 3 B3 61

Boat Tours

Canal cruises are the mainstay of the tourist industry in Amsterdam and they are all quite similar. There are shorter or longer tours, and options include cocktails, candlelit dinners, jazz and gourmet safari dinner varieties. Some boats can even arrange a wedding ceremony. But there are some alternatives to these large glass-topped boats with muffled commentary in 10 languages. You can hire your own boat and guide of course, or sign up at Boom Chicago (p.219) for the free (but a donation is expected) St Nicholaas Boat Club tours.

The Best of Holland

020 420 40 00

Damrak 34, Centrum   www.thebestofholland.nl

One of Holland's largest tour companies, their wide variety of tours include a two-hour Amsterdam By Candlelight cruise, and their popular Canals and All That Jazz Cruise. Pick-up can be arranged from various hotels in the city. Map 3 C3 **55**

Blue Boat Company
020 679 13 70
Stadhouderskade 30, Oud Zuid   www.blueboat.nl
Conveniently located between the Rijksmuseum and Max Euweplein, the Blue Boat crews provide a variety of services including customised cruises and the facilities to get married on board. Map 11 F1 **44**

Bootnodig Boat Rentals
020 419 66 50
KNSM-laan 377, Zeeburg   www.bootnodig.nl
This company offers the opportunity to explore the country by boat, whether it's on the Amstel river, the Wadden Sea, the Ijsselmeer, South-Holland or Zeeland. They have a wide selection of boats, yachts and motorboats available. Map 1 E1

Canal Bikes
020 623 98 86
Various Locations   www.canal.nl
Take a canal tour and cycle at the same time. Pedal boats can be rented at four different locations, including the Rijksmuseum and Anne Frank Huis. Great for families, particularly those whose kids have legs long enough to reach the pedals – it's hard work.

Canal Bus
020 623 98 86
Weteringschans 26, Canal Belt   www.canal.nl
Pricey, but convenient, hop-on and hop-off boat that takes in most of the major tourist spots in the city on its three routes

with 14 stops. A one-day ticket for adults is €18, for children (aged 4 to 13) it's €12. Map 9 D4 **45**

Canal Hopper
Weteringschans 26-1 hg, Canal Belt

020 626 5574
www.canal.nl

The Canal Hopper is an electric, open boat operating at weekends in the summer. There are two routes, from the Westerpark to the city centre and another touring the architecture of the Eastern Docklands. If you are travelling with a group, it is worth considering hiring one (captain included) for a private tour. €120 an hour.

Classic Canal Charters
Czaar Peterstr 147hs, Oost

020 421 08 25
www.classiccanalcharters.com

A tour in one of these charmingly authentic boats is a stylish way to wind your way through the city's canals. Dinner, group and special event trips are also available. Map 1 E2

Holland International
Prins Henrikkade 33A, Centrum

020 622 77 88
www.hir.nl

Cruises leave the harbour every 15 minutes between 09:00 to 18:00 and every half an hour from 06:00 to 21:00. Candlelight lunch and dinner cruises are also available. Map 3 C2 **48**

Kooij BV Rederij
Rokin 125, Centrum

020 623 38 10
www.rederijkooij.nl

Amsterdam's largest boat tour company, regular tours set off twice every hour, as well as candlelit tours and private boat hire for groups. Commentary is in eight languages. Map 6 C3 **49**

Lindbergh

020 622 27 66
Damrak 26, Centrum
www.lindbergh.nl

Daily one-hour cruises are offered each day at 30 minute intervals. Candlelight and dinner cruise options also available.
Map 3 C3 50

Lovers

020 530 10 90
Hendrikkade 25 – 27, Centrum
www.lovers.nl

Lovers run daily cruises every hour from 09:00. Night cruises including dinner are offered daily in the summer and on Wednesdays, Fridays and Saturdays in winter. The museum and shoppers boat has a fixed timetable and you can buy a day pass (€17) that includes discounts on museum entry fees. Map 3 B2 51

Smidtje

020 670 60 67
Ruysdaelkade 174, Oud Zuid
www.smidtje.nl

These charming and comfortable canal boats cruise Amsterdam's old city centre, and with prior arrangement, up the Amstel or to the windmills at Zaandam. Boarding is normally at the Rijksmuseum or on Ruysdaelkade but other arrangements can be negotiated. Map 12 C3 52

Wetlands Safari

020 686 34 45
Various Locations
www.wetlandssafari.nl

From May to the middle of September, you can take a tour with Wetlands Safari to explore scenic Waterland villages and the landscape that inspired Rembrandt and Ruysdael. The safari uses canoes and rowing boats to explore the wetland areas outside the city.

Bus Tours

You can squeeze in a lot of Dutch highlights in one day on a bus tour with one of these companies. The Dutch tourist board also produces a booklet with many tour options.

The Best of Holland   020 420 40 00
Damrak 34, Centrum   www.thebestofholland.nl
One of the biggest tour companies, the wide range of tours covers all the main attractions of the Netherlands. Map 3 C3 35

Key Tours   020 200 03 00
Paulus Potterstrat 8, Oud Zuid   www.keytours.nl
Key Tours offer tours of the city and dinner cruises, as well as exploring further afield to places like Edam, Volendam, Marken, Delft, Den Haag and Belgium. Map 11 F2 96

Diamond Tours

Amsterdam is famous for diamond trading, and it's possible to have a guided tour around a diamond factory, where you can get an insight into the cutting and polishing process, and then select a diamond and setting to suit your taste. Try Coster Diamonds (020 305 55 55, Paulus Potterstraat 2-6), Stoeltie Diamonds (020 623 76 01, Wagenstraat 13-17), Van Moppes Diamonds (020 676 12 42, Albert Cuypstraat 2-6) or Zazare Diamonds (020 626 27 98, Weteringschans 89).

Kids' Activities

A visit to a farm or petting zoo – a kinderboerderij (www.kinderboerderijen.nl) – is fun for kids and there are many right in Amsterdam. Just south of the city, Ridammer Hoeve and its biodynamic goat farm in Amsterdamse Bos is a great day out. Or spend a night on a Dutch farm (www.boerenbed. nl). Amsterdam kinderboerderijen can be found in the south-east: De Bijlmerweide (Provincialeweg 46a, 020 695 11 49) and De Gliphoeve (Ganzenhoefpad 8, 020 690 01 43); in De Pijp: De Dierenpijp (Lizzy Ansinghstraat 82, 020 664 83 03); and in Rembrandtpark: De Uylenburg (Staalmeesterslaan 420, 020 618 52 35). See also For Families on p.17.

Walking Tours

There are several companies offering walking tours of Amsterdam, as well as themed itineraries (following Rembrandt's trail, for example) for which you can buy a particular map or go in a group with a guide. See the company entries below, or visit the tourist board, which organises several.

You can also check out ARCAM (p.89), which publishes audio and bike tours, or Amsterdam City Walks (06 18 257014, www.amsterdamcitywalks.com), which has a range of 90 minute tours for €8 per person.

Free tours are on offer from New Amsterdam Tours (www. newamsterdamtours.com), which meets throughout the year, in all weathers, at 11:00 and 15:00 next to the tourist information office in front of Centraal Staation. The guides wear red T-shirts. If you want to do it yourself with Amsterdam on your i-pod, try www.audiocitytours.com or www.walki-talki.com. Or for a few addresses to check out on a walk around the Canal Belt, see Grand Canal Lowdown on p.72.

The Best of Holland
Various Locations
020 420 40 00
www.thebestofholland.nl

Lots of options. Its tour of the Red Light District is fun, frivolous and only slightly naughty. Tours are also available further afield, throughout Holland and Belgium.

Amsterdam City Tours
Various Locations
06 14 295174
www.amsterdamcitytours.com

Tours include the Daily City Walk, Cannabis Tour and Dark Amsterdam Tour (including the Red Light District).

Red Light District Tour
Prins Henrikkade 94-95, Centrum
020 623 63 02
www.dewallenwinkel.nl

This two and a half hour tour takes visitors through the past present and future of the Red Light District. Starts from Café Schreierstoren near Centraal Station. Map 3 D2 57

Urban Home and Garden Tours
Meet near Rembrandtplein, Canal Belt
020 688 12 43
www.uhgt.nl

A chance to see some stunning 17th to 20th century homes and gardens around the city. Tours last up to to three hours, and run from April through to October. Map 5 A2 58

Tour Operators

Amsterdam City Tours (Bus)	06 14 295174	www.amsterdamcitytours.com
The Best of Holland	020 420 40 00	www.thebestofholland.nl
Holland International	020 622 77 88	www.hir.nl
Key Tours	020 200 03 00	www.keytours.nl

Sports & Spas

Active Amsterdam

Whether exploring the city by bike, enjoying a quiet sail, or easing your cares with a soothing massage, Amsterdam offers a myriad of delights.

Almost every sport you can imagine is available in Amsterdam whether you want to join in or just watch. Football is a national passion, of course (this is the land of Johan Cruyff and Marco van Basten), though it can be tricky getting a ticket to watch Ajax dazzle their opponents at the ArenA (half an hour by metro from Amsterdam Centraal). Check the website (www.ajax.nl) for last-minute opportunities.

When spring comes, the parks are immediately full of people playing games or just enjoying the sunshine and warm weather. The Dutch are world champions at speed skating and a great place to try it from November to February is the Jaap Eden complex (www.jaapeden.nl). If skating on little wheels is more your thing, hire some blades in Vondelpark (www.vondeltuin.nl).

One of the best ways to see the city is by bike. You can see a lot more, a lot quicker, and there are well-marked cycle paths almost everywhere. Just watch out for the people who think the bike paths are footpaths. There are also cycle paths through the countryside connecting towns and villages, as well as along the North Sea coast (p.104) through the dunes and nature reserves. If you don't have your own bike, there are many rental shops where you can get one (see the table on p.42), and several companies offer tours in and out of the city (see Bicycle Tours on p.110).

Conservatorium

Anything to do with water is also much enjoyed. Taking a tour on the canals (p.111) is common for visitors, while sports such as rowing and sailing are also popular. Another great way to relax on the water around Amsterdam is to have a sail on the Ijmeer. If you want to swim, try the elegant Zuiderbad (020 678 13 90, Hobbemastraat 26), or De Mirandabad (020 546 44 45, De Mirandalaan 9), which is great for kids, with tropical pools, slides and wave machines. And with the sea only an hour or so away, activities like surfing (p.128) and kitesurfing (p.124) are easily accessible, with instructors if you need them.

There are also countless ways to pamper yourself in Amsterdam, whether you're looking for a spa treatment, Pilates class or bikini wax, and there are new spas and salons popping up all the time. The holistic health sector is also widespread, with meditation and other types of massage and relaxation techniques available privately or in holistic centres.

On The Water

Soak up some rays on a beach, go for a pleasurable sail on a yacht, or try the exhilarating sport of kitesurfing.

Amsterdammers have a unique selection of 'urban beaches' available to them, and the city is only around half an hour away from some of the country's finest seaside resorts. Canal tours are the best way to see the city and plenty of companies offer tours (p.111). You can also get involved and sail yourself on various types of boats, including luxury yachts. Heading out of town, you can always catch a wave in the surfing havens of Scheveningen or Zandvoort, or canoe in the peace of the Dutch countryside.

Beaches

In the city centre you can find the unusual artificial beach called Amsterdam Plage (p.96), to the north-west of Centraal Station. The most central beach in Amsterdam, NEMO Beach (p.95) is on top of the NEMO science centre, with fantastic views over the city; it also has a cafe serving snacks. Just a 15 minute tram ride from Centraal Station, Blijburg aan Zee (p.94) is famous for both its beach and its parties.

Out of the city, beaches on the North Sea coast (west of Amsterdam) include Bloemendaal, which offers a party atmosphere with bars and nightclubs; the exclusive Wijk aan Zee, great for surfing; and Zandvoort, the easiest to get to, by train from Amsterdam. For the locations, see the Amsterdam Overview map on the pullout map in the back.

Bloemendaal aan Zee

Noord Holland   www.bloemendaalaanzee.goedbegin.nl

It is not just the temperatures that are hot all along this stretch of coastline, four kilometres north of Zandvoort. This is the spot where the hip and happening head to catch the rays and DJs on the beachfront. During the summer months Bloemendaal is where the party starts early and finishes late. The two best-known clubs are Republiek and Woodstock. Take the train from Amsterdam to Haarlem, then bus number 81 to Bloemendaal aan Zee.

Wijk aan Zee

Noord Holland   www.wijkaanzee.info

Further up the coast, just north of the Noordzeekanaal, Wijk aan Zee is even trendier – perhaps because it's just that much more exclusive. It's a smaller version of the Bloemendaal beach, with a more relaxing vibe. This area is known to have some of the best surf in the country, and the best surfers. It's a relaxing place to hang out, catch a wave or check out some of the kite and windsurfing exhibitions. The place to be is Timbuktu.

Zandvoort

Noord Holland   023 571 79 47
                 www.info-zandvoort.nl

Zandvoort is only 30 minutes west of Amsterdam by train. The beach area is set up to provide almost anything that any sunbather could want, including food, drinks, beach umbrellas, changing rooms and nude bathing sections. It's less hip than the more fashionable Bloemendaal, but quite a few of the Bloemendaal set are now returning.

Canoeing

The best way to enjoy the waterways around Amsterdam is to get out on the water. The scenery looks completely different from this perspective and you can also venture out into the more natural regions just outside the city either with a guide or on your own.

Just to the north of Amsterdam, Waterland is a nature resort set in a traditional rural landscape of grassland that is home to cows, small villages, old farms and a lot of water. Canoeing is an excellent way of discovering the area on pre-set courses, with maps available from the VVV tourist information centres, the visitors' centres of Staatsbosbeheer (State Organisation for Nature Preservation) or through the organisation's website (www.staatsbosbeheer.nl). One of the places you can rent a canoe is the 'pontje van Ilpendam' (www.pontveer-loots.nl) at the Noordhollands Canal, the canal that connects Amsterdam to the North Sea.

Kitesurfing

If you get a kick out of kitesurfing, Holland is a great place to enjoy your sport. Just a short distance from Amsterdam, a lot of the Dutch coastline is highly suitable for adrenaline junkies. Log on to www.windjunks.nl/kitespots for information on almost 60 spots for catching the wind and waves in the Netherlands and the Benelux.

Some of the easiest places to get to on the North Sea (just a short train ride from Amsterdam through Haarlem) include Bloemendaal aan Zee, Zandvoort and Wijk aan Zee (see p.123), which are ideal for kitesurfers.

Clockwise from top: Kitesurfing on Zaandvoort beach, canal bikes on Singelgracht, canal by kayak

The Flying Pig Beach Hostel
071 362 25 33
Parallel Boulevard 208 2202, Noordwijk   www.flyingpig.nl

The Flying Pig Beach Hostel is right on one of Holland's beautiful beaches, Noordwijk. It is a relaxed place to hang out, meet new people and do surfing of all kinds. The beach is large and spacious enough to launch your own kite. If you don't have kitesurfing equipment, you can rent it. Lessons are available for beginners and for experienced kitesurfers.

The Spot
023 571 76 00
Noordstrand 23a, Zandvoort   www.gotothespot.com

The Spot starts students out on the beach with kite control lessons. Once you can make the kite do what you want it to do, the rest is easy and you can fly over the water enjoying the excitement of kitesurfing. It offers courses of one, two or more days and each lesson lasts about four hours. Lessons consist of theoretical knowledge, safety, getting to know your kite, launching, landing, and steering the kite. Courses begin in May.

Sailing

Amsterdam is famous for its waterways, and there are plenty of opportunities to view the city and the surrounding area from onboard various types of boats. For more details about cruising the city's canals, a favourite tour for many visitors, see Boat Tours on p.111. If you are looking to venture further afield or hire a boat, you can sail to places like the Ijmeer lake, the Wadden Sea or the IJsselmeer (see the companies on p.128).

Geldersekade

Bootnodig Boat Rentals

020 419 66 50

KNSM-laan 377, Zeeburg

www.bootnodig.nl

If you need a boat for a special occasion, company trip, meeting a party or just to cruise through Amsterdam's canals, Bootnodig is a great option. It has boats, yachts and sailing vessels to suit every need, and anyone can sail. It arranges everything for you, from the captain down. Arranging a boat is easy; the website is in English and the company will gladly answer any questions you have about destinations and catering. Map 1 E1

Klipper Avontuur

020 683 88 65

Van Diemenkade 14, Westerpark

www.avontuur.nl

Klipper Avontuur (Clipper Adventure) offers different types of sailing outings; one is around three hours (more of a dinner cruise), others last for five or eight hours or even a whole weekend. It caters for the entire event so all you have to do is enjoy being on the open water. There are a variety of boats you can choose from and you can book individually or as a group. Map 1 C2

Surfing

While Holland is no Hawaii or Australia, the beaches on the North Sea coast have some decent waves and there is an enthusiastic surfing community. Some people say don't bother bringing your board in the hope of catching some waves, but if you already have it with you, or want to rent, there's plenty of fun to be had. You'll have to leave Amsterdam and go either west or south, but there are many

Beach on North Sea, north of Zandvoort

popular spots on the beaches, where there are surf shops that usually open during the summer months (including Dfrost below). All have a wide variety of surfing gear, lessons and people willing to help if you're thinking about trying your hand at hangin' ten. See also Beaches (p.122), and in particular, Wijk aan Zee (p.123).

Dfrost Surf'n Beachculture
Passage 33, Zandvoort

023 573 00 38
www.d-frost.nl

Dfrost offers surfing classes as well as equipment like surfboards, wetsuits, swimboards and windsurfing gear. It provides instruction and the friendly staff can answer any questions you have. Haven't tried golf surfing? You can here. Half an hour from Amsterdam, it's open seven days a week from 12:00 to 22:00, June to September.

Spas & Well-Being

Enjoy refreshing treatments at one of the best spas. An aromatic massage or a quiet reflective meditation will add to your sense of contentment.

Health spas are a popular luxury getaway in the Netherlands, with many people enjoying a weekend retreat at an out-of-town spa. There are numerous health spas situated along the coast and also inland, and Newport Health & Spa in Huizen is one of the closest and most popular with people from Amsterdam. In the city itself, luxurious day spas with a vast array of treatments have recently begun to crop up. Massage and meditation are widely available, and are an ideal way of relaxing those tired limbs and replenishing the spirit.

Health Spas

AVEDA Dayspa

020 794 93 66
www.dayspa.nl

Laan der Hesperiden 90, Oud Zuid

This new spa is an oasis of tranquillity and a haven for the mind, body and spirit. Not only is it aesthetically beautiful with its airy, light foyer, but the friendly, highly trained staff put you in a serene state of mind from the moment you enter. Using natural products, it offers nurturing treatments for the entire body based on AVEDA's Elemental Nature philosophy, drawing from ancient plant-based healing traditions to balance infinity, air, fire, water and earth. Map 1 C4

AVEDA Dayspa

130

Hammam

020 681 48 18
Zaanstraat 88, Westerpark   www.hammamamsterdam.nl

In this traditional bathhouse, women of all nationalities and cultures are welcome. In the bathing sections there are areas with different temperatures and a Turkish steam bath. There are two rooms where you can rejuvenate after bathing, a place to enjoy snacks and refreshments, and other areas where you can enjoy massages or use a sunbed. The basic treatment (which includes entry, soaping, scrubbing and mud pack) costs €25. Entry is €15 for those over 12 years. Map 1 C2

Newport Health & Spa

035 523 33 04
Labradorstroom 75, Huizen   www.newport-health-spa.nl

This spa is approximately 40 minutes south-east of Amsterdam by car in the Hotel Newport near the Gooimeer in Huizen. The treatments are derived from Ayurveda, an ancient

Indian philosophy. The spa facilities include health food bar, terrace on the harbour, solarium, steam room, whirlpool, health club and much more. A half-day spa package costs €110, while the full-day option is €189. Reservations are advised at least three weeks in advance, even if you are staying at the Hotel Newport.

Sauna Deco
Herengracht 115, Canal Belt
(Grachtengordel)
020 623 82 15
www.saunadeco.nl

This old-fashioned art deco mixed sauna is situated in the heart of Amsterdam. It boasts two saunas, a Turkish steam bath, a cold water immersion pool with jet stream, hydromassage, a tanning booth and an outdoor terrace. Light meals and beverages are available, and also various beauty treatments at Salon Deco (020 330 35 65). A full-day beauty package for €115 includes robe and towels, coffee or tea, basic facial treatment, sauna facilities, 25 minute massage and lunch. Map 2 F4 🛈

Sento Spa & Health Club
Marnixplein 1, Jordaan
020 330 14 44
www.sento.nl

The newly opened Sento Spa & Health Club is an exclusive addition to Amsterdam's urban surroundings. It boasts a stunning contemporary Japanese interior and ultra-modern facilities. The spa offers a variety of day treatments which last four hours and include lunch, priced between €85 and €139 per person. You can choose between different combinations or separate treatments such as relaxing facials, hydromassage, floating, hot stone massage and other sublime experiences. There is also a rooftop terrace and swimming pool. Map 5 B1 2

Massage

Corpus Rub

020 416 50 55
Van Breestraat 72, Oud Zuid
www.corpus-rub.com

Corpus Rub is an elegant and inviting massage studio with black walls, soft white furnishings and waxed wooden floors. As you're being massaged in the light, private, garden-facing room upstairs, lie back and listen to gentle, soothing lounge music. If it's raining, the therapeutic sound of the raindrops on the skylight adds to the experience The studio also offers two massage rooms downstairs with a candle-lit, peaceful, subdued ambience. A 60 minute massage is €57, but you can also go for the ultimate – 90 minutes for €80. Map 11 E4 3

doctor feelgood

020 620 15 70
Czaar Peterstraat 116, Zeeburg
www.doctorfeelgood.nl

Esther van der Plas, a licensed and certified massage therapist from New Mexico, USA, has opened 'doctor feelgood', her bright and cheerful massage parlour, in Czaar Peterstraat. Enjoy unwinding in this intimate little place with its clean, calm, white and grey, stylish interior. Esther is very much in demand after years of experience working all over the world, and she offers top quality therapeutic massage using natural products, aromatherapy, and hot or cold mud packs with every customised treatment. Map 1 E2

The Health Company   020 471 07 56

Cornelis Schuytstraat 48, Oud Zuid

The Health Company is a quaint, small shop known for its wonderful natural cosmetics, food supplements, books and beautiful gifts. It now also offers various types of revitalising massage and energy therapy in the cosy little house in the back garden. On offer are bio-dynamic massages, Ayurvedic consultations and aura-soma colour therapy. A new healing evaluation therapy called NES (Nutri-Energetics Systems) can scan for bodily imbalances. Map 1 C4

Koan Float Centre   020 555 03 33

Herengracht 321, Canal Belt
(Grachtengordel)   www.koan-float.com

This centre offers a unique method of relaxation: floating on a bed of water in a womb-like, soundproof fibreglass capsule, complete with light, mood music and two-way intercom. To complement your floating session you can further de-stress with one of its many massages including relaxation massage, shiatsu, foot reflexology and rebalancing. A 60 minute float costs €37.50 and 60 minute massage €47.50. A combination of both costs €82.50. Map 6 B4 4

Meditation

Brahma Kumaris Spirituele Akademie 020 624 02 05

Haarlemmerdijk 137, Jordaan   www.bksa.org

This is a branch of the Brahma Kumaris World Spiritual University (www.bkwsu.com), an international organisation founded in India with over 7,000 centres in 103 countries. Leave the busy Haarlemmerdijk and enter an oasis of serenity and peace in the centre of Amsterdam. In this calm sanctuary Raja Yoga meditation is taught, which aids your spiritual awareness. Classes are free, but donations are always appreciated and there's never any pressure. Contact the centre for a course schedule and programmes. Map 2 C2 🖰

Expanding Minds   06 12 366956

Centrum De Roos, P.C. Hooftstraat 183,
Oud Zuid   www.expandingminds.nl

Gisele Burnett gives weekly meditation classes in English at Centrum De Roos in Vondelpark. Her method of teaching is practical and grounded, using a western approach to what many consider an eastern practice. The classes offer a peaceful, supportive environment for meditation and reflection. Classes are held every Wednesday evening from 18:30 and 20:30, and cost €10 per class. Map 11 E2 🖰

Maitreya Instituut   020 428 08 42

Brouwersgracht 157-159, Jordaan   www.maitreya.nl

The Maitreya Instituut is open to anyone interested in learning about Tibetan Buddhism and meditation. The coordinator of its Amsterdam branch teaches group classes in English to newcomers to meditation and those who want to further their meditation skills. The institute also offers weekend courses and other activities. Meditation classes are €2.50 per class and €22.50 for a 10 class series. See the website for more details. Map 2 C2 🖸

Shopping

Shopping Amsterdam

From bustling markets in bicycle-strewn squares to galleries with eye-catching art, Amsterdam offers a vibrant choice of retail environments.

Shopping in Amsterdam offers something for everyone, from the top fashion names located on the P.C. Hooftstraat to the high-street chains on the Kalverstraat; from the small independent boutiques nestled in the Jordaan, to the mile-long market in Albert Cuypstraat, where fresh produce, household goods and textiles are all brought together in a vibrant mix of scent, sound and colour.

There are thousands of shops in Amsterdam attracting huge numbers of shoppers every day and the Calvinistic roots of Dutch culture have created a thrifty consumerism where value for money is a top priority. But style is also important, so outlets that supply affordable design are cherished. Vintage clothing, furniture made out of recycled products, cosmetics that have not been tested on animals, organic food and fair trade products are also all part of the shopping scene.

Prices compare well with other European cities and many American destinations and are just above those in Hong Kong. For visitors from non-EU countries, tax-free shopping is available at many central stores when you spend €50 or more. Since the local value-added tax (BTW) is usually 19% (or 6% on consumer basics and items such as flowers or books), this is a significant incentive for big-ticket items.

Sunflowers at Bloemenmarkt

Look out for the sign on the shop front and keep your receipts to get cash back at the airport. See www.vatfree.nl or www.globalrefund.nl for more details.

Department stores and tourist outlets will almost certainly take credit cards, but keep some liquid funds handy for smaller boutiques. If you are on the hunt for a bargain, look out for the racks marked 'uitverkoop', 'korting' and 'kopje', or shops that offer 'kassa korting%' on selected items. There are generally big sales after the Sinterklaas season (which finishes on 5th December), and summer sales that start in June.

Amsterdam shopping culture is very relaxed and that includes the opening hours. Many shops don't open until 10:00, even in the centre on a Saturday, and Mondays are very quiet. If shops in the Jordaan and Negen Straatjes are open at all, it often won't be until mid-morning. Shopping hours are

extending to Sunday, however, and on Thursdays many shops stay open until 21:00.

If you have hired a car, don't even think of driving it into the centre: parking is limited and expensive. It's usually easier to travel by bike, on foot, or by public transport. If you want a mall experience there are some excellent shopping centres with parking facilities on the outskirts of the city: Boven t'Y Winkelcentrum is a mix of high-street shops, supermarkets and an open-air market, Woonmall Villa Arena, and next to it, ArenA Boulevard, are centres for electronics and furniture. In any case, the distance between shopping zones is very manageable so if you don't fancy lugging your carrier bags from one end of Leidsestraat to the other, you can always hop on a tram.

So what to take home? Amsterdam is well known for diamonds, so if you fancy something sparkly, visit one of the polishing factories or a jeweller (see Diamond Tours p.115). Holland is also known for the tulip trade; tulip bulbs and a myriad of other plants are available all year in the flower market on the Singel. You'll spot Delft blue china in the souvenir shops all over the city, from cutesy girls in clogs and Dutch caps to 17th century tiles, but if you want a really special piece of china (and your pockets are deep) head for the Spiegelkwartier and browse the many specialist antique shops there.

This section offers a guide to the shopping hotspots in the centre, where you'll find the best markets, the main shopping malls and the major department stores. It also tells you where to go for the city's finest offerings in art, books, clothes, design, flowers, food and souvenirs.

Antique and curiosity shops

Hotspots

Amsterdam is famous for its trading past. A stroll through the city's commercial hubs will prove the Dutch have lost none of their commercial flair.

Beethovenstraat

Oud Zuid   www.beethovenstraatamsterdam.nl

This is an upmarket shopping street, located in Oud Zuid close to Amsterdam RAI Exhibition Centre and Amsterdam World Trade Center. There is a mix of shops on offer including exclusive fashion, interior furnishings, garden accessories and specialist food shops. You can find the latest Bang & Olufsen sound system or Villeroy & Boch dinner service alongside grocery shops. Get there with tram 5 or 24. Paid parking is available if you go by car. Map 1 D4

Haarlemmerstraat & Haarlemmerdijk

Near Centraal Station, Jordaan

Starting at the end of the Singel, where the Stubbe's herring stall stands on the bridge, these streets run west to Haarlemmerplein with an eclectic mix of shops, from women's fashion (including natural fabrics and vintage) to food and foodie related accessories including many specialist delis (French, Portuguese, Spanish, Moroccan, Thai…). Unusual chocolate combinations can be tasted at Unlimited Delicious (020 622 48 29, www.unlimiteddelicious. nl) or buy chocolate Amsterdammertjes (little posts) at Beune (020 624 83 56). For tea and coffee try 't Zonnetje (020

623 00 58, www.koffietheeenkruiden.nl) or bakers such as Bakkerij Mediterrane (020 620 35 50) or Vlaamsch Broodhuis (020 528 6430, www.vlaamschbroodhuys.nl). The wines and tapas in the Hollandaluz Spanish delicatessen (020 330 28 88, www.hollandaluz.nl) are delicious, and Kaasland cheese shop (020 422 17 15, www.kaasland.com) offers a range of cheeses, which you can try before you buy. If you feel like lingering, there are plenty of restaurants and cafes in the neighbourhood. Take a seat on one of the terrace cafes near the Herenmarkt and watch the world go by. The area is a short walk from Centraal Station (10 minutes or so) to pick up a great picnic. Map 2 E2 ⬛

Jordaan
West of Canal Belt

There is a village atmosphere in Jordaan, especially on Saturdays with people at the markets clutching loaves of bread and implausibly long cut flowers. The Noordermarkt (p.150) has an organic market on Saturdays and a flea market on Mondays, with fabrics on sale down Westerstraat. Retail gems can be found on the cross streets (dwaarstraatjes) running between the main

Affordable Art

At one time, Jordaan's cheaper rents attracted struggling artists who couldn't afford anywhere else and it's still an area packed with galleries. They 'specialise in the various' as one owner put it, but check out famous forger Geert Jan Jansen (Nieuwe Spiegelstraat 61 in the Museum Quarter), who sells collectible reproductions of Picasso, Matisse or Appel.

canals that dissect the neighbourhood. These narrow lanes hide fashion boutiques, vintage furniture stores and gift shops such Ans Wesseling in Petsalon (020 624 73 85), who sells designer caps and hats, or the lovely La Savonnerie (020 428 03 23, www.lasavonnerie.nl) for its Amsterdam soap. On the Rozengracht, the main road bisecting the Jordaan, Kitsch Kitchen (020 622 82 61, www.kitschkitchen.nl) and SPRMKT (020 330 56 01, www.sprmkt.nl) are fun designer emporiums, and the whole area is also stuffed with small galleries. Take your time to wander round this restful and authentic district (see Maps 2 and 5) and stop for a huge slice of apple tart at Café Winkel on the corner of the Noordermarkt. Map 2 C4

Kalverstraat
020 627 69 05

Heiligeweg, Canal Belt (Grachtengordel)   www.kalverstraat.nl

Kalverstraat is the pedestrianised centre of the central shopping district, and on weekends it gets packed. Running south from the Dam to Spui then onto the Muntplein, it is served by all the trams running down Rokin and Nieuwe Zijds Voorburgwal. All the main high-street stores are located here, so it's great for affordable fashion, shoes, accessories, cosmetics, CDs and books. One entrance to the Kalvertoren mall (p.152) is on this street, opposite V&D. Maison de Bonneterie (Rokin 140-142, 020 531 34 00) is close by, opposite the side street Heiligeweg, whose shops offer a slightly more exclusive tint. For a leisurely break, Café Luna (Kalverstraat 96, 020 622 28 05) is situated about halfway along. Alternatively, slip off to the cafe terraces on the Spui or brace yourself for the crowds with a coffee in posh department store De Bijenkorf (p.152). Map 6 C2

Clockwise from top left: Artistic fashion display, bookshop, Shoe Baloo

Negen Straatjes

Canal Belt (Grachtengordel)　　　　　www.de9straatjes.nl

The Negen Straatjes are the nine little streets connecting the grand canals, forming an unmissable, quirky district full of antiques, fashion and speciality shops housed in architecturally charming surroundings. You can pick up a handy free map of the area from many of the shops and you will need it – even locals find it tricky to remember exactly what is where. Wolvenstraat is a hotspot for vintage clothing with Laura Dols (020 624 90 66, www.lauradols.nl) on both sides of the street, with vintage dressing-up-clothes for kids as well – circus master outfit anyone? Runstraat has notable food stops including one of Amsterdam's best cheese shops, De Kaaskamer (020 623 34 83), and an organic baker. Continue down the street (now Huidenstraat) to savour the best croissants in Amsterdam at elegant Pompadour (020 623 95 54). Map 5,6,9

Nieuwendijk

Nieuwendijk, Canal Belt (Grachtengordel)　　www.nieuwendijk.nl

The Nieuwendijk runs from the Dam towards Centraal Station, and ends at the Singel. Close to the Dam, it feels like Kalverstraat with more high-street names – C&A, Free Record Shop (020 622 80 34), and two branches of H&M (0900 1988) – but as you get closer to the Singel there is a definite change towards shops designed for tourists coming into town from the train station. In between the ubiquitous souvenir shops selling T-shirts and Delft blue are coffeeshops, outlets selling smoking paraphernalia, sex shops selling everything from the titillating to the bizarre, and amusement arcades. Map 3 B4

Pieter Cornelisz Hooftstraat

Oud Zuid   www.pchooftstraat.nl

PC Hoofstraat has the greatest collection of designer shops in Amsterdam. If you need Louis Vuitton luggage or a Mont Blanc pen, an outfit from Chanel or a Cartier watch, it's all here, sumptuously displayed. The designer names ensure a steady flow of the rich and famous. While you may find it hard to park your car among the Porsches and Harley Davidsons, the nearby underground parking on the Museumplein is very convenient and almost as chic as the shopping area. At the top of the PC Hooftstraat is the Van Bearlestraat, which also has a fine selection of exclusive fashion. Map 11 E2

Spiegelkwartier

Canal Belt (Grachtengordel)   www.spiegelkwartier.nl

The area on Spiegelgracht and Nieuwe Spiegelstraat offers art and antique lovers everything they could wish for, with over 70 specialist shops. Whether you collect modern art, Chinese porcelain, rare coins or Louis XV furniture, it's all here. You can browse to your heart's delight and spend to the depth of your pockets. Prices range from just a few euros for pretty prints of Amsterdam up to items costing many thousands.

Take a stroll around Jaski Art Gallery (p.82) or Gertrude D Galleries (Nieuwe Spiegelstraat 33, 020 624 76 81) to appreciate the variety of works on offer in this creative city. As this area is in the heart of the Canal Belt, there is no direct public transport, but you can take tram 2, 5, 6, 7, 10 or 12, or bus 26, 65, 66 or 170 to the Rijksmuseum and walk. Map 9 D3/D4

Markets

The vivid colours of the markets capture the spirit of Amsterdam: it's a city blossoming with variety and life.

Albert Cuypstraat Markt
Albert Cuypstraat, De Pijp

The biggest and most central of the city's markets, Albert Cuypstraat Markt has around 300 different stalls, so there really is something for everyone. It's filled with quality food, cheese, flowers, clothes, music, household items and a range of textiles, all at low prices. The market is open every day except Sunday from 09:00 to 17:00. Several tram routes take you directly to this market, including 4, 16, 24 and 25. Map 1 D4

Amstelveld
Off Prinsengracht, Canal Belt (Grachtengordel)

Located between Utrechtsestraat and Reguliersgracht, this square is central and two markets are held there. On Mondays there is a plant and flower market from 09:00 to 18:00, and once a month on Fridays in the summer there is an antique and collector's market. To get there by public transport, take tram 4 to Keizersgracht, the metro to Weesperplein, or bus 355, also to Keizersgracht. Map 10 A2 2

Bloemenmarkt
Singel Canal Belt (Grachtengordel)

The famous floating flower market, with each stall on a separate barge moored on the Singel, seems like a tourist trap

Clogs

as you can get masses of souvenirs, blue and white china, and clogs and wooden windmills. The market is open every day, and is very busy with sightseers. The quality of the flowers and bulbs, however, is superb. This market is central – take tram 1, 2, 4, 5, 9, 16, 24 or 25 from Centraal Station. Map 9 D1 🔢

Dapperstraat Markt
Off Wijttenbachstr, Indischebuurt

Previously voted 'the best in the Netherlands', Dapperstraat is one of the oldest in town. It is a busy and multicultural centre, with prices much lower than those in centrally located shops. It is great for basic items, and is enjoyable just to wander around, Get there by taking tram 3, 7 or 10 to the Dapperstraat stop, or by bus 22, 37, 59, 120 or 126. If you're taking the train go to Muiderpoort Station. Map 1 E2

Nieuwmarkt

Near Gelderskade, Centrum

Every Saturday there is an organic market in this atmospheric square in the heart of old Amsterdam, 10 minutes' walk from Centraal Station. On Sundays in the summer there is a large antique market in the same square. If you don't feel like walking from the Centraal Station, take the metro line one stop to Nieuwmarkt. Map 3 E4 4

Noordermarkt

Near Nooderkerk, Jordaan

The organic farmers' market each Saturday brings a breath of the country into the city. Twenty years ago this was the first such market in the Netherlands, and today it's a great place for cheese, bread and fresh vegetables. There are other products such as fresh cosmetics and pottery, and fashionistas come for a rummage through the fabrics and vintage clothing. On Monday mornings there is a flea market with antiques, collectibles and clothing. It's on the Prinsengracht at the end of the Westerstraat. Get there through Jordaan, or on tram 3 to Westerstraat. Map 2 D3 5

Postzegelmarkt

Nieuwezijds Voorburgwal, Centrum

This small market (the Stamp Market) specialises in stamps, coins and medals, and is open every Wednesday and Saturday afternoon. For collectors it's the place to go for new pieces, to trade items, or for browsing. Take any of trams 1, 2, 5, 6, 13 or 17 to the Dam stop. Map 6 B2 6

Spui

Near Kalverstraat, Centrum

The Spui is a pretty square in central Amsterdam, and there
are two markets each week. Every Friday from 10:00 to 18:00
is the book market to which traders come from all over the
Netherlands to sell rare and first-edition volumes and prints.
This specialist market is not cheap, as it is aimed at serious
collectors, but it's a great place to browse. Also worth a visit is
the art market every Sunday from March until December, from
09:00 to 18:00. Trams 1, 2, 4, 5, 9, 16, 24, or 25 from Centraal
Station will get you there. Map 6 C4 🔟

Waterlooplein Market

Waterlooplein, Centrum

This daily flea market is a mix of antiques and plain old
second-hand items. There are old theatre costumes and
army uniforms, prams that could have been used by Queen
Wilhelmina, and vintage crockery. Full of curiosities, it's a great
place to browse around. Waterlooplein is behind the Stopera,
and you can take the metro or tram 9 from Centraal Station to
get there. Map 3 E4 🔟

Westermarkt

Near Keizersgracht, Canal Belt (Grachtengordel)

This market specialises in textiles, although you can also get
fresh market produce, clothing and accessories here. It is only
open on Mondays, and best visited in the mornings as in poor
weather the stall holders will pack up early. Located close to
the Jordaan, take tram 3 to get there. Map 5 E2 🔟

Malls & Department Stores

Upmarket department stores and two malls offer luxury, value and plenty of choice, whether for exclusive gifts or just to escape a Dutch downpour.

de Bijenkorf

0900 0919
Dam Square, Centrum
www.debijenkorf.nl

This Dutch institution has its flagship Amsterdam store on the corner of Dam Square in a beautiful building that opened in 1914. The style is certainly not dated, however. The accent is on excellent and attractive design whether in home furnishings, children's toys or fashion. In the run up to the Sinterklaas celebrations it's an exciting place to take children. The store is wonderfully decorated and Sint himself appears regularly on his throne and holds audience to enthralled youngsters. On 6 December (when Sinterklaas has left for Spain) up go the Christmas decorations. There are good sales, particularly the 'drie dwaze dagen' (three crazy days) if you are visiting in the autumn, when there are huge price reductions. Map 6 C1 **10**

Kalvertoren

Kalverstraat 212-220, Centrum
www.kalvertoren.nl

With entrances on Heiligeweg, Kalverstraat and the Singel, this shopping mall (opened in 1997) is an attractive airy space on four floors, with a central lift and escalators. It has a full range of interesting places to shop, from international

Fresh produce

names in fashion such as Replay, Mango, Dockers and Hilfiger Denim, to cosmetics, home furnishings, sportswear and luxury chocolates. There are small food outlets scattered throughout the mall, but the Café and Brasserie Kalvertoren is a bit more special, offering a rooftop view of the city as you eat. It's a great place to spend a couple of hours on a cold and wet Amsterdam day. Map 6 D4 **11**

Magna Plaza   020 626 91 99

Nieuwezijds Voorburgwal 182, Centrum   www.magnaplaza.nl

This was the first shopping mall to be opened in Amsterdam, and is centrally situated behind the Dam Palace in the former Central Post Office building. It is a beautiful setting in which to shop for designer fashion, jewellery, gifts and cosmetics. If you really want to indulge yourself you can have a massage at the Back to Life Massage Company on the top floor, or get a new hairstyle at the branch of Toni & Guy also located there. The mall is very easily reached by tram lines 1, 2, 5 and 17, which pass behind the Dam Square. Map 6 A1 **12**

Metz & Co   020 520 70 20

Leidsestraat 35-36, Canal Belt   www.metzenco.nl

This exclusive store, first established in 1740, was granted the title 'Purveyor to the Royal Household' in 1815. With a tradition of supplying the international elite, at the beginning of the 20th century it became the sole agent for Liberty of London in the Netherlands, Europe and Dutch overseas colonies. Its location in the middle of the main tourist area surrounded by other upmarket high-street shops, with easy access by trams

Magna Plaza

1, 2, and 5 on Leidsestraat, makes it hard to resist browsing for a while. The rooftop cafe offers great views. Map 9 C2

V&D

0900 235 8363

Kalverstraat 203, Canal Belt   www.vroomendreesmann.nl

This chain of department stores was established 120 years ago, and you will find a V&D (Vroom & Dreesmann) in most big shopping centres. You are guaranteed a good selection of competitively priced products, be it kitchen utensils, household fabrics, home accessories, luggage or fashion. It has its own brand, as well as international names. The company recently launched the brand 'Fair Trade Original' and actively encourages global social responsibility. V&D is known for its innovative 'La Place' restaurant chain. The La Place formula offers fresh and healthy fast food which can be taken away or eaten in attractive surroundings. Map 6 D4

Where To Go For...

Art

To get a flavour of Dutch contemporary art go to the prestigious art society, Arti Amicitiae (020 623 35 08), on the Rokin. International auction houses Sotheby's (De Boelelaan 30, 020 550 22 00) and Christie's (Cornelis Schuytstraat 57, 020 575 52 55) are both represented in the city. Stroll down Nieuwe Spiegelstraat and check out Jaski Art Gallery (p.82) or wander through Negen Straatjes. For sculpture visit De Beeldenwinkel on Berenstraat (020 676 49 03). Affordable art can be found at Art Cash & Carry (Westerstraat, 020 330 23 70), and the many galleries in Jordaan are also worth browsing, particularly when artists open their ateliers to the public. You can also visit one of the weekly art markets such as Torbecke Plein or Spui (p.151).

Books

There are many specialist and second-hand bookshops, almost all of which have English language titles, but if you love books then the place to look first is Spui, home every Friday to a book market. Spui also has a large branch of Waterstone's (Kalverstraat 152, 020 638 38 21) and the American Book Center (Spui 12, 020 6250 55 37), which has a wide range of books and press. Athenaeum (020 514 14 60, www.athenaeum.nl) stages many literary events and has a huge selection of international art, fashion and design magazines, and newspapers. Around the corner on Koningsplein is the city's largest bookshop, Scheltema (020 523 14 11). In Jordaan the English Bookshop (Lauriergracht 71, 020 626 42 30) is a lovely meeting place.

Clothes

Amsterdam's department stores have good clothing sections; de Bijenkorf (p.152) and Maison de Bonneterie (Rokin 140, 020 531 34 00) stock plenty of designer brands. European high-street labels (H&M, Zara, C&A) can be found on Kalverstraat, as well as stylish ladies' fashion at Claudia Sträter (Kalverstraat 179, 020 626 07 08). Van Baelstraat and P.C. Hooftstraat are the old south destinations for exclusive brands including groovy Shoe Baloo (www.shoebaloo.nl). Head for Jordaan or Negen Straatjes if you want something more individual. Vintage clothing is fab at Laura Dols (Wolvenstraat 6, www.lauradols.nl), Lady Day (www.ladydayvintage.com) and Episode (www.episode.eu), or rummage at the Monday and Saturday markets. For stylish wear for men, women and kids, only available in Amsterdam, browse the rails of Exota (www.exota.com). Hot handbags can be found at Claire V (www.clairev.nl) on the Prinsengracht or Dutchies (www.dutchiesdesign.nl) in Runstraat.

Design

Witty, functional Dutch design is internationally acclaimed. The work of home-grown talent and the hottest international designers can be seen and bought from droog-at-home (Staalstraat 7B, www.droogdesign.nl) or Frozen Fountain (www. frozenfountain.nl), both of which are part gallery, part shop. For accessories rather than art, the Rosengracht in Jordaan has some interiors shops such as SPRMRKT (www.sprmrkt), and out on KNSM island you'll find Pol's Potten (www.polspotten.nl).

Flowers

Flowers are very much part of Dutch life. They are sold all over the city from canalside stalls and beautiful florist shops in every neighbourhood, and the freshness and quality are guaranteed to be excellent. Expect to pay from €12 to €30 for a bouquet which should last at least a week after purchase if you follow the florist's instructions – so yes, you can take those tulips home! Bloemenmarkt (p.148) on the Singel is the city's famous floating flower market where you can also buy many varieties of bulb, but you do need to ensure they are importable to your home country. At the Amsterdam Tulip Museum (www.amsterdamtulipmuseum.nl) near the Anne Frank Huis (p.73) in Jordaan, you can learn more about the famous bloom and buy bulbs in the shop.

Food

Dutch snacks are available all over town, particularly the ubiquitous patat (French fries) that you dunk in mayonnaise, ketchup or satay sauce: Vlaamse Friethuis on Voetboogstraat is a top spot. Fish stalls are the place to taste herring (haring), Dutch shrimps (Hollandse garnalen) or eel (paling). Whether you like your fish cut up in chunks in a bread roll or with chopped onions and gherkins, it's up to you. Popular with kids are kibbeling, which are deep-fried, battered cod chunks.

FEBO, the food-from-the-wall chain, is a Dutch institution. At these all-day vending machine venues, you put in a coin and out comes a frikandel (offal posing as frankfurter), bitterballen

Cheese shop

(croquettes of doughy mash and beef or veal), kaas souffle (deep-fried breaded cheese) or other sordid snacks.

For exotic breads, and savoury and sweet treats, try one of the Vlaamse Broodhuis outposts (www.vlaamsebrookhuis.nl). For cakes and pastries, you need a 'banketbakker'. For cheese, renowned shops include De Kaaskamer (Runstraat) and Kaasland (Haarlemmerstraat 2, 020 422 17 15).

Traditional Dutch sweets (snoepjes) include liquorice drops that come in many guises, including both salty and sweet. And no Dutch experience would be complete without little boxes of chocolate hundreds and thousands (hagelslag) to top a slice of bread at lunchtime (or breakfast or dinner) for grown-ups as well as kids. The chunkier flakes, called vlokken, are even more delicious. All are available in supermarkets.

Speciality food from across the globe can be found in the Dapperstraat and Albert Cuypstraat markets, and De Pijp generally is the place to heard for Surinamese, or indeed any world food. Throughout Amsterdam there are European and Asian food stores and delis like Feduzzi Mercato Italiano (Scheldestraat 63, 020 664 63 65) and Patisserie Kuyt (Utrechtsestraat 109, 020 623 48 33). For more on Amsterdam's food see Going Out (p.162) and Food & Drink (p.224).

Souvenirs

The first thing you notice as you walk down Damrak from Centraal Station is the number of tacky souvenir shops, all stuffed to the rafters with 'typically Dutch' souvenirs. At the Bloemenmarkt flower market (p.148) on the Singel, you can stock up on many items from tulip bulbs to fridge magnets, all quite cheap. For clogs, clomp to De Klompenboer (020 623 06 32), the wooden shoe factory just off the Nieuwmarkt.

The luxurious surroundings of de Bijenkorf (p.152) or Magna Plaza (p.154) near Dam Square are good when it's raining. What about a metre-long tube of Droste chocolate pastilles perhaps, or a bottle of Jenever? Museums are always good for classy souvenirs. The Van Gogh Museum (p.84) has everything from posters to leather handbags with Vincent Van Gogh motifs. The Amsterdams Historisch Museum (p.65) has another good selection including magnetic gevelstenen, the tablets on Amsterdam houses indicating the profession of a previous occupant. The tobacco trade made the Netherlands rich and the extraordinarily beautiful cigar shop P.G.C. Hajenius (020 623 74 94) on the Rokin is worth a look even for non-smokers.

Chocolates are another great idea. Posh chocs can be found at branches of Puccini (Singel, www.puccini.nl), the wonderful Pompadour (Huidenstraat) or Unlimited Delicious (www.unlimiteddelicious.nl). If you are in town during the Sinterklaas season, chocolate letters are available at supermarkets like Albert Heijn. Their shelf life can be a little limited, so you might end up eating them before you go home. Cocoa has a longer life though and the tins are very decorative.

Amsterdam has a long history in the diamond trade, and there are several factories offering guided tours to demonstrate their cutting and polishing techniques (see Diamond Tours on p.115). You can also visit the world's first diamond exchange (www.diamantbeurs.org).

Going Out

Eet Smaakelijk!

Amsterdam is the laidback party capital of Europe. Alongside its famous coffeeshops is a great cafe scene, eclectic eateries and a buzzing nightlife.

Amsterdam's lively cafe and bar scene is a highlight for many, and venues tend to be full round the clock. Daytime can be just as busy as night; the large student population, sizeable part-time workforce and regular influx of partying visitors means there's a constant crowd in search of refreshment.

There is good eating to be had in the city and if it's quantity you're after, you'll easily be able to satisfy your appetite; many Dutch chefs like to present menus of three, four or five courses to their diners.

Delicious staples typically devoured by the locals are salmon, sliptong (a type of sole), garlicky shrimps, homegrown lamb and all manner of stews, and there is a good range of international choice too.

The Dutch eat quite early in the evening, although dining out later is becoming more common – you'll find that some restaurants now serve up until 01:00. Cafes and many restaurants open for lunch, or stay open from 10:00 or 11:00 until late in the evening. Many restaurants are closed on Sundays or Mondays, so it's worthwhile calling to check.

Eating Out

Although Amsterdam has been a hub of multicultural dining for many decades, with influences of cuisine from former colonies such as Indonesia and Suriname, simplicity rules the roost. The city is slowly catching up with other European capitals in terms of such culinary fashions as freshly grown organic food, Asian fusion and modern local cuisine, but sandwich bars and cafes are the most popular. The authentically Dutch brown cafes are famed for their atmospheric interiors, complemented by their traditional food and beer (see p.167).

The king of Dutch sandwiches is the tosti, a melted affair of edam or gouda with ham. Fish stalls offering raw herring and a selection of shrimps and mackerel dot the cityscape, while the eetcafe (p.169), or 'eating house', is still the best value in the mid-range category – expect to pay between €10 and €20 for a three-course dagschotel (daily menu) consisting of meat, veg and potato. In the winter, erwtensoep (split pea soup) is everywhere. Also called snert, it includes chunks of sausage and is served with rye bread. Stamppot (mashed pot) is another winter comfort food where potatoes are mashed with a green vegetable such as kale (boerenkool), or endive (andijvie) and served with smoked bacon on rye bread. Spring delights include white asparagus with ham and egg sauce. For more on Dutch food, see Food & Drink on p.224.

The Yellow Star

This star highlights places which merit extra praise. It could be the atmosphere, the food, the cocktails, the music or even the crowd – whatever the reason, they're a little bit special.

By European standards, good restaurants in any culinary category here are slightly expensive; for a decent three-course meal, including wine, expect to pay from between €25 to €40 per person, and easily more. If you're seeking a more refined dining experience like Michelin-starred French or Japanese, or clever organic or fusion, you also have plenty of options in Amsterdam's burgeoning foodie scene. Eet Smaakelijk! (Bon Appetit!)

Drinking

The Netherlands is a beer-lover's delight. There are over 1,200 drinking venues in Amsterdam, not bad for a population of less than a million. From the traditional brown cafes (right) to swanky lounge bars, funky locals to English-style pubs, you won't have to look far to find one. And as soon as there's a smidgen of sunshine, even if it's cool and windy, Amsterdam's bars and cafes put tables and chairs outside.

For a civilised evening, you might want to steer clear of the lively Leidseplein and Rembrandtplein, which are magnets for tourists and stag parties. And for those who want to dance the night away, late bars and clubs are scattered around town (see Nightclubs, p.171). If you're planning a full-on night on the town, prepare for things to start late, and to finish a lot later – nightclubs don't really get going until midnight.

Coffeeshops

Amsterdam is Europe's marijuana-smoking capital. At the city's famous coffeeshops, which are controlled and licensed by the government, cannabis is permitted to be openly sold to the public and smoked on the premises. Adults over 18 are allowed to buy five grams. The options available are usually shown on a menu with photos or a chalkboard. They are not normally noted for offering food, and are not allowed to serve alcohol.

Bulldog Palace (020 626 51 85, Leidseplein 17) is the most well known and is the first stop for most coffeeshop tourists, while Bluebird (020 622 52 32, St Antoniebreestraat 71) has a 1970s style cosy atmosphere. Grey Area (020 420 43 01, Oude Leliestraat 2) is tiny and hip, and movie buffs will love De Dampkring (020 638 07 05, Handboogstraat 29) which featured in *Ocean's Twelve*. For a mellow atmosphere with lounge seating and incense, try De Rokerij (Lange Leidsedwarsstraat 41), which has a Tibetan feel with Nepalese and Hindu artwork. Rusland (020 627. 94 68, Rusland 16) is a large, multi-level coffeeshop, which some claim was the city's first.

Brown Cafes

Known in Dutch as bruine kroegs, and sometimes referred to as brown bars, a real kroeg is likely to be around 200 years old and have walls plastered with posters dating back almost as far. They get their name from their dark appearance, richly coloured wood and subdued lighting. Some of the oldest and most popular in Amsterdam include Elsa's Café (p.205), De Druif (p.211), Café Hoppe (020 420 42 20, Spuistraat 18-20) which has been serving beers since 1680, and Café Chris (020 624 59 42, Bloemstraat 42), a favourite with locals since 1624, apparently including Rembrandt. Café de Oranjerie (020 623 43 11, Binnen Oranjestraat 15hs) has walls full of posters, plenty of board games and good quality pub food.

Venue Directory

The venues in this chapter are grouped by area, but if you're after a particular type of food or bar, the directory below will help you find what you're looking for.

Italian	Roberto's	p.202
	Yam Yam Trattoria-Pizzeria	p.217
Japanese	Yamazato	p.203
Mexican	Los Pilones	p.189
Middle Eastern	Bazar Amsterdam	p.199
	Maoz Falafel	p.176
	Nomads	p.189
	Shibli Bedouin	p.178
Moroccan	El Kasbah	p.216
Portuguese	Restaurant Portugalia	p.190
Seafood	Café Potgieter	p.216
	Eenvistweevis	p.210
	Visaandeschelde	p.203
Spanish	Mucho Más	p.205
	Vamos a Ver	p.202
Steakhouses	Gauchos	p.175
Surinamese	New Draver Restaurant	p.206
	Nieuw Albina	p.201
Turkish	Kismet Eethuis	p.201
Vietnamese	Little Saigon	p.216

Bars

	Bourbon St Blues	p.190
	Bubbles & Wines	p.178
	Café Cuba	p.179
	Café Pakhuis Wilhelmina	p.211
	Café Pieper	p.191
	De Druif	p.211

Centrum

Sipping wine on the banks of the Amstel, enjoying a classy Sunday brunch or an evening in a sultry cocktail bar – variety is the spice of life in the heart of the city.

Perfect for a delicious Italian-style breakfast, whiling away your afternoons with a latte sat on picturesque waterfront terraces, or chilling to mellow jazz in a brown cafe, Centrum offers you it all on a plate. The heart of the city, it's chock-a-block full of attractions, including trendy nightclubs and bars, classy steakhouses, Chinatown, as well as traditional Dutch eateries and the uniquely hedonistic experience of Supperclub (right).

Venue Finder

Cafes

Café de Jaren

Nieuwe Doelenstraat 20-22   020 625 57 71

This spacious grand cafe and restaurant is in a magnificent old three-storey bank building on the Amstel river. Most people come to relax on the splendid waterfront terrace or for a light lunch from the healthy salad bar upstairs. The cost of lunch is average, but dinner prices are a bit steeper. It attracts an eclectic mix of arty, trendy types, students and tourists. Map 6 E3 **26**

i Supperclub

A unique experience where diners lounge on beds while an extraordinary cabaret performs around them. Restaurant, bar, club, international creative brand – it's a legend. Jonge Roelensteeg 21, 020 344 64 00.

Esprit Caffe

Spui 10   020 622 19 67

This cafe is known for tasty American cuisine like juicy hamburgers, but also does chicken and avocado wraps, a variety of healthy salads, and tummy-warming tomato soup with dill among other offerings. The choice is immense, the portions are generous and prices are reasonable. Try for one of the tables outside on Spui Square.   Map 6 C4 **27**

Puccini

Staalstraat 21   020 620 84 58

Mornings in this sunny, modern Italian cafe kitchen are a sheer delight, as you're met by the aromatic scent of freshly baked croissants and rich, Italian brewed coffee. The fluffy scrambled eggs with fresh herbs, toast and salad come with salmon or warm ham for a mere €7.50. Their sandwiches are a feast for the eyes as well as the palate.   Map 6 F3 **28**

Restaurants

De Roode Leeuw

                                           Dutch

Damrak 93-94   020 555 06 66

Near to the Dam monument lies a very old-fashioned Dutch institution combining a restaurant, cafe and hotel. The menu offers many local favourites, such as several varieties of hotchpotch (mash filled with cabbage, kale or spinach and topped with bacon). The staff are playful and patient with kids. The buffet breakfast is open to the public, and the quality and value is very good.   Map 6 B1 **30**

d'Vijff Vlieghen
Dutch

Spuistraat 294-302   020 530 40 60

Foreigners and locals adore this restaurant and come back for more than just seconds – the quality just doesn't let up. This is New Dutch cooking at its finest in one of the most beloved spots in the city, (The Rembrandt Room) that reeks with authenticity and old world charm. The daily changing seasonal menu with an excellent array of wines awaits the uninitiated. A little expensive, but worth every cent.   Map 6 B4 **31**

Flo Amsterdam
Eetcafe

Amstelstraat 9   020 890 47 57

The local franchise of the famed Paris brasserie chain, this place is warm and inviting, and the menu specialises in the cuisine of the Alsace region – a knockout hybrid of German and French delicacies. Highlights include artichokes in vinaigrette, grilled quail salad with asparagus, and the choucroute – a stew of sauerkraut, pork and bacon. For dessert, try a sorbet or the lemon tart with berries.   Map 6 F4 **33**

Gauchos
Steakhouses

Spuistraat 3   020 625 72 72

Gauchos is a top-class steakhouse with six locations serving up beef that has been grazed on the Argentinian pampas. Chimichurri oil is used on the sizzling grills, and the aromas that waft through the restaurant will build up your appetite. For starters, try the ceviche, shrimps or scallops. Mains include rump, fillet, sirloin, rib-eye or churrasco – it's all authentic stuff, so sit back, relax and enjoy.   Map 3 B3 **36**

Greetje

Peperstraat 23

Dutch

020 779 74 50

With a charming, old world atmosphere, this is the home to new Dutch cuisine. Venture down into an alcove billed as 'the mayor's table' for lucky diners who can look outside through the huge glass window at the bicycles and canal boats. A typical Dutch menu may include blood sausage with apple compote, white asparagus with Hollandaise sauce, and egg white and ham. A wonderful place to eat.

Map 4 A4 **32**

Maoz Falafel

Muntplein 1

Middle Eastern

020 420 74 35

No one can beat Maoz for quality falafel. This clean little corner haven serves up healthy, 100% pure vegetarian fastfood treasures. Choose from falafel on plain or wholewheat pita with an array of toppings. It can be a bit messy to eat so you should bring plenty of tissues or take it away (there are less than 10 seats inside). Map 6 D4 **37**

Nam Kee

Zeedijk 111-113

Chinese

020 624 34 70

Amsterdammers have been raving over Nam Kee for over a decade – it's one of the top Chinese restaurants in the city. In reality, it is a good price for a quality pitstop, and it's noted for its peking duck with plum sauce (you really can't go wrong for €12). Ask for the piquant spices the Chinese use. It does a decent spare rib, although at times you may get more fat than pork. Service is snappy and fast. Map 3 D2 **29**

Clockwise from top left: Cool modern eatery, homely Dutch restaurant, d'Vijf Vlieghen

Shibli Bedouin
Middle Eastern

Oudezijds Voorburgwal 236
020 554 60 79

The first and only replica in Europe of a Bedouin night out in the Sahara, a belly dancer graces the floor while you smoke a shisha water pipe. The five-course set menu with wine, beer and soft drinks will set you back €60. Eat with your hands, starting with cold dishes laced with spices, then move on to vine leaves stuffed with minced lamb, chicken and prunes.

Map 6 D1 35

Wintertuin
International

Dam 9
020 554 60 25

This classic old world room (the Winter Garden) at the Krasnapolsky Hotel is a national monument. It takes you back to the end of the 19th century when wrought iron decor and glass-covered arboretums were all the rage. The Sunday brunch served here is more like a Sunday dinner, so it's not to be missed. The set-price menu includes champagne. Map 6 C1 34

Bars

Bubbles & Wines
Nes 37
020 422 33 18

A secret cave of bottled treasures that caters to the discerning pallet, Bubbles & Wines is tucked away behind the Rokin on the theatre-rich Nes. The long, thin bar has a tasteful interior with a soothing atmosphere, and serves up a wonderful assortment of wines and champagnes by the glass or bottle. Worth a visit for anyone interested in wines. Map 6 C2 38

Café Cuba

Nieuwmarkt 3   020 627 49 19

Located on the fashionable Nieuwmarkt, Café Cuba is incredibly popular in summer. It has a large terrace, decent service and affordable prices. They offer a good range of cocktails by glass or pitcher. The crowd tends to be Dutch students and after work drinkers. There's no food available but the area has a lot of great restaurants nearby. Map 3 E4 39

Gollem

Ramsteeg 4   020 676 71 17

Gollem is a true haven for beer lovers. It was the first specialised beer cafe in Amsterdam, and is still one of the best, with over 200 beers to choose from. If you'd like to try something from the tap, the knowledgeable staff will be happy to give you a tester and the history of the beer before you commit to a full glass. The crowd is varied with a good bunch of regulars who know how to appreciate good beer. Map 6 B3 40

Harry's

Spuistraat 285   06 21 558300

Harry's is a small cocktail bar located near Spuiplein. Styled after cocktail bars in New York, it is small but well decorated, with a large table at the front and a few small tables at the back and upstairs. The cocktails are fantastic but pricey, beginning around €8. The staff are impeccably dressed and the service professional, but attention to detail means orders can take a while to appear. Map 6 B4 41

Jazzcafé Alto

Korte Leidsedwarsstraat 115   020 626 32 49

The place to go for jazz fans; don't expect the old school stuff though. It's a very popular venue so if you want to grab a seat, get there early – you'll probably not be the only one waiting. The interior is in the style of a simple brown cafe. The crowd is very mixed, with a liberal sprinkling of different nationalities and age groups. Prices are reasonable. All in all, a safe bet for a pleasant night out if you like jazz. Map 9 C4 **42**

LUX

Marnixstraat 403   020 422 14 12

This fairly funky, arty bar is massively popular at the weekends, and busy other nights too. Its slightly later opening hours may be why, or it could be the relaxed atmosphere, sexily seedy interior design, reasonably priced drinks and retro films screened above the bar. If you want to get your foot in the door, arrive before 22:00. Map 9 A3 **43**

Wynand Fockink

Pijlsteeg 37   020 639 26 95

What began as a local distillery for liqueurs, jenever and other traditional Dutch tipples is now one of Amsterdam's best loved 'proeflokaals', or tasting rooms. It's a time machine full of magic potions; they've been distilling in the same way for over 350 years and do it very well. The walls are covered in traditional brown shelves holding mysteriously coloured bottles. The old distillery is still operating next door and you can stop by for a tour or a workshop. Map 6 C1 **44**

Nightclubs

Club 11
Oosterdokskade 3-5   020 625 59 99

Located on the 11th floor of the industrial looking ex-post office building near Centraal Station, Club 11 has spectacular views of Amsterdam from windows on all sides. Open daily for lunch or dinner, the venue transforms into a club on Friday and Saturday evenings from 22:30. The crowd is young, hip and urban, but fairly relaxed, with everyone out to have a good time. The music and the entry fee vary depending what's going on – a usual club nights cost around €12. Map 3 F1 **45**

Club NL

Voorburgwal 169   020 622 75 10

One of Amsterdam's plushest and most decadent lounge clubs, the rich interior urges you to sink back into the cushions and melt into the music. Open every night of the week, it's more lounge bar during the week. Come Thursday, however, and the mellow tunes disappear and the dancing shoes come out. Depending on the day and how late you arrive, you may not have to pay the €5 to €10 entry fee, but you'll certainly pay and pay for your drinks. Map 6 B2 46

Gay & Lesbian

Café Rouge

Amstel 60   020 420 98 81

This friendly, kitschy bar is just off the beaten path. One wall holds pictures of celebrities, while old turn-of-the-century photos in gilded frames grace another. This is a consummate locals' bar. A barmaid stands in front of a huge vase of red roses while a DJ spins old Dutch pop music and a few customers sing along. The atmosphere is very comfortable, a little like stepping back a bit in time. Map 6 E4 49

Gay Scene

Amsterdam is famous for its thriving gay and lesbian bar and club scene, which is spread throughout the centre. Some bars are clustered in areas such as Reguliersdwarsstraat (p.184), where a mixed crowd can feel comfortable. Other venues can be found all over town (see p.171).

Club Cockring

Warmoesstraat 96   020 623 96 04

While the name implies a leather scene, that's not the only thing you'll find at Club Cockring. The €5 cover gives you entry to plenty of cruising space, there's a disco in the basement, and there are even small rooms available, if necessary. It attracts a fairly diverse crowd, but maintain a mellow atmosphere. There are regular strip shows and it really gets going around 01:00 at the weekends. Absinthe is available at the bar downstairs. Map 3 C4 **71**

Cuckoo's Nest

Nieuwezijds Kolk 6   020 627 17 52

Cuckoo's Nest has the feel of a small city leather bar. The lighting is a bit brighter than usual and the crowd is very normal, not at all strictly leather. Poppy music perfectly accompanies the several screens of run-of-the-mill porn. The main room is a good size and there's a cellar with darkrooms and a regular stream of men going in and out. A place to visit on a bar crawl, but maybe not end the night at. Map 3 B3 **50**

The Queen's Head

Zeedijk 20   020 420 24 75

This bar is situated at the beginning of the busy Zeedijk, in the oldest part of Amsterdam, it provides a cosy venue to sip drinks and look out of the back windows onto the canal while listening to hip music. They have regular bingo with Amsterdam's most famous transvestite, Dolly Bellefleur. Well worth stopping in for a biertje. Map 3 D3 **51**

Canal Belt & Jordaan

Nestled amid the networks of canals lie some of the city's hottest nightclubs and restaurants, and a lively cafe scene.

With famous nightclubs such as Melkweg (p.192) and Paradiso (p.192) drawing some of the world's best bands and DJs and setting the beat for the rest of the city, this is the perfect spot for some nocturnal neon excitement. Reguliersdwarsstraat is home to several gay bars, while classy restaurants like Beddington's (p.186) and Ron Blaauw (p.190), offer fine dining.

Venue Finder

Cafes	★ Buffet van Odette	p.185
American	Hard Rock Café	p.189
Belgian	Belgica	p.186
Eetcafe	Baton	p.186
Eetcafe	Goodies	p.188
French	★ Ron Blaauw	p.190
Indian	★ Balraj	p.185
Indonesian	Cilubang	p.188
International	Beddington's	p.186
International	Eat at Jo's	p.188
Mexican	Los Pilones	p.189
Middle Eastern	Nomads	p.189
Portuguese	Restaurant Portugalia	p.190
Bars	Bourbon St Blues	p.190
Bars	Café Pieper	p.191
Bars	Gespot	p.191

Cafes

Buffet van Odette

Herengracht 309, Canal Belt   020 423 60 34

Charming owner Odette conjures up a scrumptious scrambled egg breakfast served with possibly the best croissants in Amsterdam. Delicious sandwiches are under €5; quiche, salads, home-made cakes, apple pie and brownies make this a favourite stop for both locals and tourists. It has a lovely canal-side picture window. Map 6 A4 🔳

Restaurants

Balraj   Indian

Haarlemmerdijk, Jordaan   28 020 625 14 28

Indian cuisine is not very common in Amsterdam, but when it's done properly – as it is here, people flock to it. Balraj has been in business for over 30 years, and while the restaurant is a simple affair, it has an extensive curry menu (you can order any degree of heat) and all types of naan breads. The lamb sag is delectably cooked. Those on a budget will appreciate the prices. Cash only. Map 2 C2 **6**

Baton
Herengracht 82, Canal Belt

Eetcafe

020 624 81 95

The cobble-stoned terrace of this Lilliputian cafe overlooks one of the prettiest canals in town. A good lunch stop for a break after walking around the centre, try the oversized salads loaded with chicken and bacon, or the Dutch tosti, a melted delight of cheese and ham on toasted bread – large enough for a satisfying meal. Map 2 F4 **4**

Beddington's
Utrechtsedwarsstraat 141, Canal Belt

International

020 620 73 92

It's hard to pin down or put a label on the sublime creations you can expect here. One night you'll be blessed with a crab and asparagus entree, on another sushi of grapefruit with braised and grilled duck. Diners jealously eye the next table to peek at what they decided not to order. Staff are very knowledgeable about the far-reaching wine list, and every week there's a new modern menu. Map 10 B1 **8**

Belgica
Kleine-Gartmanplantsoen, Canal Belt

Belgian

020 535 32 90

Belgica is a relaxed cafe-cum-brasserie – the zinc bar and the antique replica espresso maker are a throwback to the days of the crooners. The Belgian-style fries with mayonnaise are

Cafes and bars in Leidseplein

thickly cut. You can order anything on the menu at any time, so if you're in the mood for a hot plate of steak after an all-nighter, this is the place to go. Map 9 B4 **3**

Cilubang
Runstraat 10, Canal Belt

Indonesian
020 626 97 55

Tuck into an East Javanese selection of rice and spices, as you enjoy an intimate dining experience, at once romantic and otherworldly. The various assorted rijsttafel (rice table) comprises of 15 to 28 dishes that can be enjoyed in this rustic 16th century house. Wayang Golek puppets hang on the walls and seem to sway to the Gamelan music that wafts through the air. Map 9 A1 **7**

Eat at Jo's
Marnixstraat 209, Jordaan

International
020 638 33 36

Attached to the famous concert venue Melkweg (p.192), Eat at Jo's serves up good home-cooking to regular customers, pre-gig diners and visiting rock stars. A rock'n'roll joint with a care-free spirit, there is an alchemy of combinations available: spinach soup with cheese, burritos with tofu and beans, and curry. Individual requests can be dealt with, and it's great for vegetarians. Map 5 C1 **9**

Goodies
Huidenstraat 9, Canal Belt

Eetcafe
020 625 61 22

This tiny spot on the nine streets uses wooden picnic tables inside and outside to foster an atmosphere of relaxation. Order a hearty lunch, soup and bread fresh from the oven, or the sandwiches that topple over they're so large. House wine is reasonably priced and there are fixed-price menus. Map 9 B1 **5**

Hard Rock Café
American
Max Euweplein 59/61, Canal Belt
020 523 76 25

The burgers don't get any better or bigger in Amsterdam. The views overlooking the Vondelpark and the hurly burly of the canals keep the young ones entertained. Desserts come in large portions and the fudge brownie is just too much for one person. Reservations recommended. Map 11 E1 **2**

Los Pilones
Mexican
Kerkstraat 63, Canal Belt
020 320 46 51

A small place with a big reputation, Los Pilones provides some of the best dishes you'll find outside Mexico. The cacti fried with steak can be washed down beautifully by a Corona. Enchiladas, tacos and quesadillas leave no space for desserts. There's a kids' menu, and a wide selection of cocktails. Dining alfresco off the busy Leidsestraat offers some respite from the shop-till-you-drop crowds. Map 9 C2 **10**

Nomads
Middle Eastern
Rozengracht 133-I, Jordaan
020 344 64 01

A magical lounge bar and restaurant, Nomads attracts the young and fashionable into rooms that are split into sections with seating on high cushions. Cocktails ooze style: strawberry martinis or cosmopolitans in long glasses and the champagne flows like water. A set three-course menu is served with tasty Arabic bread as you lounge on the sofas. Map 5 D4 **11**

Restaurant Portugalia
Kerkstraat 35, Canal Belt

Portuguese
020 625 64 90

Even though Portugalia is located in the area around the ultra-touristy Leidseplein, the food makes it worth a visit. It's a family-run enterprise where customers are made to feel at home. All manner of seafood is available. The traditional salt cod, served everywhere in Portugal, can also be found here, presented with a bechamel sauce. Map 9 B2 12

Ron Blaauw
Kerkstraat 56, Canal Belt

French
020 496 19 43

In all categories of what makes a restaurant great, Ron Blaauw deserves all the accolades he has won. A typical menu of eight courses for lunch is an outstanding testament to his ability. Scallops rolled like sushi and topped with a mousse of wasabi mustard and caviar will send you to heaven. Service here exceeds the norm, the wine list is exceptional, and the lunch menu is reasonably priced for the calibre. Map 9 B2 71

Bars

Bourbon St Blues
Leidsekruisstraat 6-8, Canal Belt

020 623 34 40

Despite the rather kitsch appearance, this place feels old and authentic. It has attracted some big names, from Sting to the Rolling Stones. Budding musicians are welcome to join the jam nights on Sundays, Mondays and Tuesdays. The crowd tends to be a bit older and quite Dutch, but very ready to let their hair down. Map 9 C3 13

Café Pieper

Prinsengracht 424, Canal Belt   020 626 47 75

A true Amsterdam institution, Café Pieper has been serving
up beer and jenevers since 1665. The atmosphere is
comfortingly old; the glass in the windows appears ancient
and the pictures of an older Amsterdam on the walls add to
the effect. In the summer you can enjoy the canal-side terrace
while watching boats pass by. Cash only. Map 9 A3 **14**

Gespot

Prinsengracht 422, Canal Belt   020 320 37 33

Beneath Gespot the restaurant you'll find a little gem of a bar.
Cosy and beautifully designed, the bar is a great place for a
pre-dinner drink or an afternoon by the canal. The service is
great and the cocktails better. The restaurant serves lunch
and dinner and there are also snacks available. You may spot
a few well known Dutch faces. Map 9 A2 **15**

Nightclubs

Jimmy Woo

Korte Leidsedwarsstraat 18, Canal Belt   020 626 31 50

A feat of design and elegance, Jimmy Woo is the ultimate
in chic. It's difficult to get into, so call ahead and try get on
the guest list. As a result, the club is full of beautiful girls and
sharp media types. The dark interior is dotted with lounges
and sleek furniture, while the bar serves fabulous (pricey)
cocktails. Downstairs is a dancefloor with amazing lighting.
The music varies in style. Map 9 B3 **16**

Melkweg

Lijnbaansgracht 234a, Canal Belt   020 531 81 81

An Amsterdam staple, Melkweg is not just about clubbing but also draws fantastic (international) bands, art exhibitions and media installations. It's a little on the scruffy side, but the crowd largely depends on what's happening. You can expect to pay from €5 to €50 depending on what you're going to see or hear. Club nights are usually €10 (you'll have to pay an extra €3 for the compulsory membership fee). Map 9 A3 **17**

Paradiso

Weteringschans 6-8, Canal Belt   020 626 45 21

Disguised as a church just off Leidseplein, Paradiso is a cultural icon in Amsterdam and shows run the gamut from punk and poetry to hard house. It attracts some of the world's biggest and best bands. Club nights usually start around 23:00 and finish around 05:00. Entry costs from €5 to €25 (excluding membership fee of €2.50). Map 9 C4 **18**

Rain

Rembrandtplein 44, Canal Belt   020 626 70 78

One of the new breed of clubs that isn't happy being just one thing, Rain is a restaurant, club and bar. The club side of things happens mostly on Friday and Saturday evenings. Its location makes it quite popular and a queue can form quickly from around 23:00. The overall look is very subtle, with a modern lounge style and an oriental influence. This is not a club for the hardcore dancer, but is a good option for a cocktail. Map 6 F4 **19**

Sugar Factory

Lijnbaansgracht 238, Canal Belt   020 624 10 12

In contrast to other nightclubs, Sugar Factory bills itself as a night theatre and every night seems crazier, stranger and more beautiful then the last. Club nights vary from disco to Brazilian beats and the cultural shows cover everything from cabaret to supercharged poetry sessions. The bar stretches the length of the dancefloor and you can also chill on the balcony if you're danced out. Map 9 A3 20

Gay & Lesbian

ARC

Reguliersdwarsstraat 44, Canal Belt   020 689 70 70

ARC is a very modern, sleek bar with a hip young crowd and cute bar staff. It serves mainly cocktails, but finger foods are available. The crowd is mixed almost to a fault, but ARC is still clearly gay. It's often very busy, but if you arrive early you can get a seat looking out onto the garden. Alternatively, go out onto the pavement to enjoy your drinks. Map 9 D1 21

Cafe 't Leeuwtje

Reguliersdwarsstraat 105, Canal Belt   020 622 25 77

One of the newest offerings in Amsterdam is the very small, but bustling, Cafe 't Leeuwtje (pronounced 'uht' Leo-chuh). It's a very female-friendly place and the crowd often overflows out onto the street. It has a very 'old Amsterdam', friendly, party atmosphere. There's free soup on Tuesdays and free coffee on Sundays. Closed Wednesdays. Map 9 E1 22

Going Out

Canal Belt & Jordaan

Habibi Ana

Leidsedwarstraat 4-6, Canal Belt   06 21 921686

Billed as 'the first and only Arabic gay bar in the world,' Habibi
Ana is a little bar off Leidseplein. The small, Middle Eastern-
style sitting area creates a cosy environment. Arabic music
and shisha pipes round out the theme and attract a good
number of Arab patrons, but non-Arabs are welcome. The
bar gets going around 23:00 and is busiest on Friday and
Saturday nights. Map 9 A2 **23**

Prik

Spuistraat 109, Canal Belt   020 320 00 02

Prik is a cute, small bar with tables out front and plenty
of inside seating. There's a large front room with a bar
and friendly staff, and a smaller, cosier room at the back
with an aquarium, where the seating fills quickly. With an
eclectic atmosphere, the mixed crowd still retains a very gay
atmosphere and Prik is the only bar in Amsterdam where you
can get a T-shirt that says, 'I love…' Map 6 A1 **24**

Pub Soho

Reguliersdwarsstraat 36, Canal Belt   020 422 33 12

Designed to look like a London pub, Soho is a large but
crowded bar with two floors. The first floor has a bar with
plenty of seating and a nice ring for cruising. A red carpeted
stairway leads to a loungy second floor where a fake fireplace
and large, comfortable chairs create a library feel. The crowd
is mixed with the great majority being men in their 30s and
40s, although anyone is welcome. Map 9 D1 **25**

The Drag Queen Olympics

194   Amsterdam Mini **Visitors'** Guide

Oud Zuid & De Pijp

With an arty, cultural feel, this area offers the unexpected, including a surreal flying saucer-shaped cafe and an urban beach where you can enjoy a romantic dinner.

This area is home to the Vondelpark, a great place to take a stroll before sampling the tapas in Het Blauwe Theehuis (p.198). The Albert Cuypstraat Markt (p.148) is Amsterdam's most popular market, and once you've shopped 'til you've dropped, you can gain an insight into the cooking methods of former colonies by trying some Surinamese cuisine at Nieuw Albina (p.201). De Pijp, a multicultural hotspot, offers a superb Japanese restaurant, Yamazoto (p.203).

Venue Finder

Cafes	De Taart van m'n Tante	p.197
Cafes	Het Blauwe Theehuis	p.198
Cafes	Strand Zuid	p.198
Cafes	Van Dam Brasserie	p.198
Chinese	⭐ Chang-i	p.200
Eetcafe	Cafe Amsterdommertje	p.199
French	⭐ Ciel Bleu	p.200
Greek	De Griekse Taverna	p.200
Indonesian	LimZz	p.201
Indonesian	Taste of Life	p.202
International	⭐ Altmann Restaurant & Bar	p.199
Italian	Roberto's	p.202
Japanese	⭐ Yamazoto	p.203

Italian cafe and gelateria

Cafes

De Taart van m'n Tante

Ferdinand Bolstraat 10, De Pijp   020 776 46 00

Famous for its wonderfully wacky cake creations and funky decor. The 'Totally Zen' Buddha cake with a fat Buddha is a classic. Not only can you buy a one-of-a-kind extraordinary wedding cake, but you can also tie the knot here. You can

even spend your honeymoon in the bed and breakfast upstairs called Cake Under My Pillow. Map 12 D3 54

Het Blauwe Theehuis

Vondelpark, Oud Zuid   020 662 02 54

Situated right in the heart of Amsterdam's most popular park, the Vondelpark (p.85), this is a funky 1930s blue flying saucer-shaped building. Spend a relaxing afternoon in the tranquil atmosphere of the teahouse or enjoy drinks and tapas sitting outside (snacks and a small dinner menu are on offer). Later on, the terrace turns into a bar. Map 11 C3 55

Strand Zuid

Europaplein 22, Rivierenbuurt   020 544 59 70

This hip urban beach is the place to be for a late breakfast, laid-back lunch or romantic dinner. The lunch menu offers sandwiches and salads, while in the evening the menu expands to include home-made pasta dishes and an array of meat and fish entrees. The kids' menu for €7.50 is just another bonus point for this super-cool hotspot. Map 1 D4

Van Dam Brasserie

Cornelis Schuytstraat 8, Oud Zuid   020 670 65 70

This place is situated along the super-chic shopping street Cornelis Schuytstraat in the Oud Zuid. It offers an array of delicious fresh salads, luxurious sandwiches, hearty soups and changing daily specials. It is almost impossible to leave without picking up a little something on the way out from the beautifully tempting traiteur. Map 1 C4

Restaurants

Altmann Restaurant & Bar
International
Amsteldijk 25, De Pijp   020 662 77 77

With a sense of flair, refined chic, charm and service, every item here is well above average. The seared scallops nestle alongside slivers of grapefruit in a sparkling duet, while their wagyu tenderloin with mango julienne will leave you orbiting outer space. Desserts are equally decadent. Their wine list is superb and a four-course meal is very reasonably priced for the quality. Map 10 E3 59

Bazar Amsterdam
Middle Eastern
Albert Cuypstraat 182, De Pijp   020 675 05 44

This cavernous former church has an intriguing blend of Middle Eastern and North African cultures. Souk-style lamps glitter with faux gems of purple, gold and green while Mosaic-adorned tables round out the colourful ambience. All meals will satisfy the hungriest appetites. In particular, the breakfast boasts yoghurt, ham, eggs, cheese, jams, pita bread and Turkish loaves. There is also a children's menu. Map 12 E1 60

Cafe Amsterdommertje
Eetcafe
Govert Flinckstraat 326, De Pijp   020 676 78 97

Eating at a warm, country-style Dutch eetcafe can be a memorable experience. With an atmosphere reminiscent of someone's home, settle in for comfort food such as halibut with caper sauce, angler fish baked in butter or lamb meatballs in a mild curry sauce. All main courses come with potatoes, salad and vegetables. There's also a reasonably priced kids' menu. Map 10 C4 57

Chang-i
Chinese

Jan Willem Brouwersstraat 7, Oud Zuid   020 470 17 00

Step into a lavish dream of a decadent Buddhist temple overlooking a Zen-like garden, where Asian chefs serve up eclectic food. Choose from innovative pan-Pacific delicacies such as beef grilled with ginger, wagyu with shallots and fois gras, and baked scallops with black bean sauce in a piquant tomato base. Portions are a little on the small side. Map 11 F4 56

Ciel Bleu
French

Hotel Okura Amsterdam, De Pijp   020 678 74 50

From the moment you sit down in this Michelin-starred restaurant, the show begins with creations that will leave your senses fizzing in overdrive. Amazing feats are on offer for main courses, and the desserts will astound. Service is personable yet professional, while the venue offers 360° views of the city. Downright fabulous. Map 1 D4

De Griekse Taverna
Greek

Hobbemakade 64-65, Oud Zuid   020 671 79 23

With staff who clearly love what they do, the food here is typical Greek taverna fare. Try the baked feta cheese with honey and thyme or the delicious giant bean salad. The Greek tomato sauce is great over grilled lamb chops and don't miss the aubergine casserole with melted feta. There's live music to kick up your heels if you're in the mood. Map 12 C4 58

Kismet Eethuis

Turkish

Albert Cuypstraat 64, De Pijp   020 671 47 68

Come here to savour inexpensive Turkish delights like the combo meals for under €10. Try the aubergine with minced lamb, courgette stuffed with lamb and rice or the delicious beef patties and rice – all come with rice, potato and ratatouille. Kismet serves Turkish wines – highly recommended is the sharp and sparkling Lal Kavaklidere rose.

Map 12 D3 63

LimZz

Indonesian

Zeilstraat 41, Oud Zuid   020 470 84 88

By day a breakfast place, yet by night it does a Jekyll and Hyde and becomes an Indonesian hotspot. With authentic, imported ingredients and spices, dishes are aromatic and flavoursome. The stark bitter herb peteh and the kemiri nuts are used with abandon, and the Gado Gado green salad is the real deal. There are no rijsttafel (rice tables) here, just fine a la carte selections. Map 1 C4

Nieuw Albina

Surinamese

Albert Cuypstraat 49, De Pijp   020 379 02 23

This hole in the wall offers cheap and appetising food, and is a great stop between the bars and nightly haunts of De Pijp. The nasi goreng comes with shrimp, pork or vegetable, while the cha siu (roasted pork) is more Chinese than South American. Roti, a Surinamese delicacy, is a filled pancake with lamb or chicken and vegetables, topped with a choice of sauces; satay, curry, sweet and sour or moksi. Map 12 C3 62

Roberto's

Italian

Hilton Hotel Apollolaan 138, Oud Zuid   020 710 60 25

Roberto's stands out because it takes liberties with the menu, whipping up original yet classic dishes from all over Italy. New chef Franz Conde is a follower of the slow food movement and procures his products directly from Italy to ensure quality. On Sundays there is a traditional Italian tea (dinner) from noon with unlimited wine for €38. Wine is available by the glass from a pretty good list. Map 1 C4

Taste of Life

Indonesian

Rijnstraat 51, Rivierenbuurt   020 644 77 86

This no-frills family run establishment offers a mix of Malay and Indonesian food, which share the same ingredients and cooking methods and presentation. They do three types of rijsttafel (rice table): small, medium and large, with ascending prices to match. Local fish is presented with peanut sauce and chicken looms large on the menu. Several vegetarian dishes are popular, from salads to a type of hazelnut with green vegetables. Map 1 D4

Vamos a Ver

Spanish

Govert Flinckstraat 308, De Pijp   020 673 69 62

Step into Vamos a Ver for a taste of Spain that will leave you begging for more. Starters can be ordered as tapas, and the paella is available in five varieties: fish, chicken, meat, seafood or combo dishes. The catch of the day is combined with prawns, shrimps and octopus in a pan streaming with spices. Service is excellent and there is a good kids' menu. Map 10 C4 61

Visaandeschelde
Seafood

Scheldeplein 4, Rivierenbuurt   020 675 15 83

The premier haunt for fish lovers. The exotic starters, such as lobster salad with duck liver swirls and truffle dressing, or smoked mackerel with marinated Portobello mushrooms, are blissful. The house offers a three, four or five-course menu. Service is excellent. If you don't mind blowing a couple of hundred euros for two, make a reservation. Map 1 D4

Yamazato
Japanese

Hotel Okura, De Pijp   020 678 83 51

Akira Oshima earned the first Michelin star ever awarded to a Japanese restaurant in Europe. That position is maintained by consistently high standards – fish for the sushi is flown in daily. Several times a year Japanese festivals are celebrated, with authentic cuisine imported for these events. Specialities are cold soba noodles with king crab or hotpots of fresh clams, or a selection from over 50 other delicacies. Map 1 D4

Bars

Kingfisher

Ferdinand Bolstraat 23, De Pijp   020 671 23 95

This is a real local bar that manages to be as inviting and relaxed during the day as it is hip and happening in the evening. Large windows complement its corner position in De Pijp, and it feels like a less-suffocating brown cafe. Good food and snacks are available and dishes change daily. Friday and Saturday evenings often feature a DJ. Map 12 C2 64

Oost, Plantage & Jodenbuurt

Full of verdant green spaces and botanical gardens, this area offers some fine Dutch cuisine alongside organic and international eateries.

A tranquil part of Amsterdam, away from the hustle, bustle and excitement of Centrum, this area boasts more sedate attractions, including an expansive park, zoo and botanical gardens. A superb Spanish restaurant, Mucho Más (p.205), offers a children's menu, while kids will love the Caribbean-style icecream in Trinbago (p.206).

Venue Finder

Cafes	⭐ Gewoon eten en meer...	p.204
Caribbean	⭐ Trinbago	p.206
Eetcafe	Elsa's Café	p.205
International	De Kas	p.205
Spanish	Mucho Más	p.205
Surinamese	New Draver Restaurant	p.206

Cafes

Gewoon eten en meer...

Beukenplein 18h, Oost   020 665 50 75

Gewoon in Dutch means 'usual', but this gorgeous traiteur/delicatessen/cafe/shop is anything but. You can relax on turquoise cushions and dark wood furniture in the tiny hip lounge and enjoy one of their 22 different daily dishes. Try the delicious pumpkin, feta, coriander and nut salad or a chicken wrap with coriander mayonnaise and chives. The patisserie offers an immense selection of decadent desserts. Map 1 E3

Restaurants

De Kas International
Kamerlingh Onneslaan 3, Watergraafsmeer 020 462 45 62

One of the first establishments to offer 100% organic food, expert chef Ronald Kunis cooks all the vegetables on the day they are harvested and they're served with meat (Waterland veal), poultry and fish, supplied from nearby farms. He has set a trend in Holland by allowing the vegetables to take centre stage, accompanied by side dishes of meat or fish. Map 1 F2

Elsa's Café Eetcafe
Middenweg, Watergraafsmeer 020 668 50 10

The favourite hangout of Ajax football team, if you're a fan, Elsa's is worth the tram ride out of the centre. It is an archetypal brown cafe, ideal for a sandwich or a pork chop with mounds of vegetables. You can easily speak to people at the bar or the next table or watch a football game. Live music at night transforms it into a folksy, offbeat setting. Map1 F2

Mucho Más Spanish
Andreas Bonnstraat 44-46, Oost 020 692 86 74

This quirky casa is brimming over with colourful flowerpots and paintings adoringly placed on the beige walls. A well-

Oost, Plantage & Jodenbuurt

rounded profusion of appetisers will satisfy even the keenest appetites. Button mushrooms in sherry and pimento-filled cheese rounds add up to excellent snacks while you're popping down some beers. For more substantial fillers, mains include turkey tapas, triple fish and grilled meat platter or paella. The three-course menu comes with delicious chocolate cake. There is a terrace outside and a children's menu. Map 1 E3

New Draver Restaurant   Surinamese
Tweede Oosterparkstraat 2, Oost   020 463 12 46

A unique and authentic place, frequented mostly by Surinamese, nothing here is watered down for local tastes. The cuisine draws from all ethnic groups in this former Dutch colony: Hindu, Javanese, Chinese and native Surinamese. The most famous dish is the moksalese, an array of meat (lamb or pork), rice or fish (cod) and rice whipped with coconut milk and spices. Map 1 E3

Trinbago   Caribbean
1e van Swindenstraat 44a, Indischebuurt   020 694 58 36

Images of sandy beaches, cool green limes, coconuts, swaying palm trees and hot spices come to mind when you say the words Trinidad and Tobago. The tender, juicy chicken with a lovely crusty batter is glazed in an orange sauce that sparkles, while the Dasheen leaves with crab, and crab cakes with slivers of chilli are both spiked with innovation. The black cake (a Trinidadian speciality) and coconut icecream will make you reel with delight. Map 1 E3

Restaurant exteriors

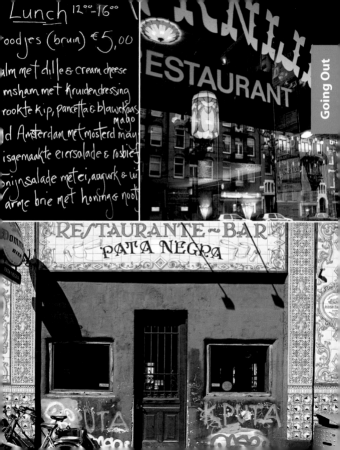

Lunch 12⁰⁰-16⁰⁰

...oodjes (brun) €5,00

...lm met dille & cream cheese

...msham met kruidendressing

...rookte kip, pancetta & blauwkaas
                              mayo
...d Amsterdam met mosterd mau

...isgemaakte eiersalade & rosbief

...onijnsalade met ei, augurk & ui

...arme brie met honing & noot

RESTAURANT

RESTAURANTE ~ BAR
PATA NEGRA

The Waterfront & Zeeburg

A vibrant and exciting place to be, the waterfront is lined with cafes and restaurants. So sit back and relax as you watch the ships come in.

The docklands area of Amsterdam is a new and exciting cultural quarter, jam-packed with artists' studios and galleries. It is in this artistic context that places like the Lloyd Hotel (p.210) in Zeeburg offer poetry readings and concerts. Other restaurants include the French, Tatin – excellent for children, and Eenvistweevis, serving up fresh seafood. The areas cafes include Star Ferry and Bagels & Beans (right), both of which offer a panoramic appreciation of the IJ harbour. While not as central as in some other areas, bars and nightclubs such as Café Pakhuis Wilhelmina (p.211) and Panama (p.211) are lively and unpretentious.

Venue Finder

Cafes	⭐ Bagels & Beans	p.209
Cafes	Mondo Mediterraneo	p.209
Cafes	⭐ Star Ferry	p.209
Dutch	Lloyd Hotel	p.210
French	Tatin	p.210
Seafood	Eenvistweevis	p.210
Bars	De Druif	p.211
Bars	Café Pakhuis Wilhelmina	p.211
Nightclubs	Panama	p.211

Cafes

Bagels & Beans
Veemkade 368, Zeeburg   020 419 46 22
A welcome addition to the up and coming docklands area,
this light and spacious waterfront cafe packs them in for
their bagels, muffins and freshly squeezed juices. Prices are
reasonable. With its waterside terrace and cheerful staff
this has already become a hotspot for young families and
professionals living on the islands. Map 1 D2

Mondo Mediterraneo
Czaar Peterstraat 174, Zeeburg   020 421 20 25
Although off the beaten track, this upmarket Italian cafe and
delicatessen definitely warrants a visit. Drop in for a heavenly
home-made lunch, or a foamy cappuccino and freshly baked
cookie outside on one of their sunny alfresco tables. The chefs
prepare fresh pastas, simple yet enticing main courses like
grilled tuna, soup, salads, and delightful desserts. Map 1 E2

Star Ferry
Piet Heinkade 1, Zeeburg   020 788 20 90
This architectural gem is a must-visit destination – the new
Muziekgebouw houses the stunning contemporary Star Ferry
cafe, with its urban cool atmosphere and incredible views in
every direction. Relax watching the harbour traffic and enjoy
a cool aperitif or snack. The day menu offers breakfast items,
plus a wide selection of sandwiches, while the dinner menu
features an eclectic mix of world cuisines. Map 1 D2

Restaurants

Eenvistweewis
Seafood

Schippersgracht 6, Zeeburg
020 623 28 94

The name means 'one fish two fish', and the fish are prepared without any superfluous additives, extras or condiments. You'll be served by the friendly staff and the chef, who chooses the fish himself daily. You'll get angler fish, sliptong (a type of sole), trout, red snapper and whatever else is the catch of the day. The tuna steaks are hamachi rose coloured, indicating the best part of the fish. Map 4 C3 **52**

Lloyd Hotel
Dutch

Oostelijke Handelskade 34, Zeeburg
020 561 36 04

The semi-art deco interior of this landmark hotel has been renovated to reflect a clean, modern style. When you order meat, fowl or fish, you can choose from one of eight sauces. Portions are large – as the side dishes alone count as a meal. Every Monday evening there are free events such as concerts, discussions, readings, art initiatives or performances. Map 1 E2

Tatin
French

Borneostraat 1, Zeeburg
020 468 51 09

When you sit on the terrace and breathe in the harbour air, you might feel like you are back in the Dutch golden age of seafaring. But you'll be brought back to earth by some of the most delicious duck or steak, served French brasserie style with a Mediterranean touch. There is a separate restaurant for children with a babysitting service and a play area. Map 1 E2

Bars

De Druif

Rapenburgerplein 83, Zeeburg   020 624 45 30

De Druif is a tiny brown cafe. It's every bit as old as it feels, with layers and layers of beer and jenever memorabilia covering the walls. The locals are friendly and chatty, especially if it's warm enough to sit outside and enjoy the peace and the view. De Druif is a quiet place to visit, away from the bustling city centre. Cash only.   Map 4 C3 53

Café Pakhuis Wilhelmina

Veemkade 576, Zeeburg   020 419 33 68

Part of the redevelopment of the warehouse district by Centraal Station devoted to promoting culture, this building houses artists, studios and the cafe. Prices are reasonable and some of the events are wonderfully offbeat; check out the Hard Rock Karaoke night. The crowd is young, hip and arty but not at all pretentious. Definitely worth a visit.   Map 1 D2

Nightclubs

Panama

Oostelijke Handelskade, Zeeburg   020 311 86 86

A bit of a trek from the city centre, Panama is a large club attracting some of the world's hottest DJs. Normal club nights cost around €10. There's also a restaurant and theatre so you can easily spend your entire evening there. The dance space is great and you'll rarely feel too squashed.   Map 1 D2

West

A less touristy part of Amsterdam, the West isn't wild, but it does offer plenty of restaurants and bars to entertain you.

Although there isn't much to explore in the primarily residential West, there's much more to the area of the city after a lot of new development, including the Westergasfabriek (p.108), a re-developed industrial complex that offers art events alongside bars, restaurants, a cinema and a theatre. Try the traditional Dutch eetcafe Bicken Eten & Drinken (p.213) on Overtoom for an authentic taste of what the Dutch really enjoy, or the gourmet Café Potgieter (p.216). It is also renowned for its Greek and Korean delis.

Venue Finder

Cafe	Toussaint	p.213
Eetcafe	Bicken Eten & Drinken	p.213
Ethiopian	Abyssinia	p.213
Indonesian	Blue Pepper	p.214
International	Bickers a/d Werf	p.214
Italian	Yam Yam Trattoria-Pizzeria	p.217
Moroccan	El Kasbah	p.216
Seafood	★ Café Potgieter	p.216
Vietnamese	Little Saigon	p.216
Bars	★ Flex Bar	p.217

Cafes

Toussaint

Bosboom Toussaintstraat 26, Oud West   020 685 07 37

This lively neighbourhood cafe has a French bistro flair, with wooden decor and candlelight making it a favourite retreat for some. The chef creates tasty sandwiches for €4 and homemade soups and salads. The dinner menu has plenty of vegetarian options. The pretty pavement terrace outside has a friendly atmosphere, and during cocktail hour (16:00 - 18:00) you can enjoy speciality tapas dishes. Map 8 E4 65

Restaurants

Abyssinia   Ethiopian

Jan Pieter Heijestraat 190, Oud West   020 683 07 92

Eating here requires mopping up the chickpeas, lentils and beef, chicken or vegetable combos with a somewhat sour pancake (like sourdough bread). The portions and the value are tremendous. The interior is quite ordinary, but it's popular with couples, if only for the idea of feeding each another by hand. The banana beer served from a coconut husk is a crowd pleaser. Cash only. Map 1 C3

Bicken Eten & Drinken   Eetcafe

Overtoom 28/30, Oud West   020 689 39 99

Located just off the Stadhouderskade, this place has changed hands many times, but at last praise can be given for the right blend of ambience, service and food. The retro 80s black interior, with touches of lilac and deep purple on the tables, is splashed against white art. The menu features fish in abundance. The tartare of tuna is unsullied, while starters include asparagus soup (white or green depending on the chef's mood) served in a warmed shot glass. Map 11 C1 **66**

Bickers a/d Werf
International

Bickerswerf 2, Westerpark
020 320 29 51

On the planks of Bickers you have a great view of life on the IJmeer. The netting on the ceiling, and pastel walls that display all manner of nautical trinkets, remind you of Holland's illustrious past. The menu is a mixture of Dutch and international favourites. The delicate mustard soup is warming, the caesar salad has real anchovies, and there are always special dishes such as guinea fowl with chestnuts. Portions are super and substantial. Lunch can be as easy as a sandwich, but the high tea is also worth a nibble. Map 1 C1

Blue Pepper
Indonesian

Nassaukade 366, Oud West
020 489 70 39

Serving up a modern version of Indonesian cuisine, Blue Pepper has gained rave reviews that are spot on and well earned. From a menu offering classic, modern and contemporary, the star chef goes the whole hog with provocative pan-Pacific combinations. The lobster thermador with Indonesian spices is terrific, or try the chargrilled Monkfish or the quail eggs served yakitori style with a spicy sambal dip. The rijsttafel (rice table) is refined and the service unabashedly understated. You'll go for seconds. Map 8 F3 **67**

Clockwise from top left: Cozy bar, Bazar Amsterdam, Dutch home cooking, stylish bar interior

Café Potgieter
Seafood
Potgieterstraat 35, Oud West   020 612 46 62

Although it looks like a cafe, this cafe is a gourmand's paradise. Everything is made using organic ingredients. Escargots, frogs' legs or silky duck rillette go nicely with the homemade bread. The seafood platter is served cold and marinated. Meat choices include Irish or Scottish tornadoes of beef, Spanish pork or a divine wagyu beef tartare. Well worth a visit. Map 8 C2 70

El Kasbah
Moroccan
Van der Hoopstraat 94, Westerpark   020 488 77 88

Rocking the kasbah isn't an option here, as you unwind puffing on a shisha pipe or chill on one of the homey sofas just like in Marrakech. Gaze up at the glittery lamps with diamond-shaped jewels or down to the mosaic-covered tables. Enjoy the tenderly prepared tajines, sweet smelling couscous dishes and chicken drizzled with cinnamon and cardamom. Generous service and portions make this your one-stop shop for a Moroccan night on the town. Map 1 B2

Little Saigon
Vietnamese
Kinkerstraat 5, Oud West   020 489 09 29

This efficient small restaurant is a newcomer to the city, and offers authentic Vietnamese cuisine without a trace of Laos, Cambodia or Thailand. Try the glass noodle salad with beef and chilli, the spring rolls (with peanut sauce), and the shrimp wrapped in rice paper. Plenty of vegetarian options are available such as tofu with garlic and ginger. Map 8 D2 69

Supperclub

Yam Yam Trattoria-Pizzeria
Italian

Frederik Hendrikstraat 88-90, Westerpark   020 681 50 97

Rub shoulders with locals in this neighbourhood trattoria, where two tiny rooms provide a cosy environment in which to indulge. The wood-burning oven tosses out the crispiest pizzas with just the right touch of cheese and tomato sauce. The menu also has veal, lamb, fish and plenty of pastas – try the linguine with porcini mushrooms. Map 5 A3 **68**

Bars

Flex Bar

Pazzanistraat 1, Westerpark   020 486 21 23

More club than bar, this is a hip, new venture with a relaxed vibe. The interior is beyond cutting edge, with sharp, sleek lines, and there are two separate areas inside; one clubby, the other more of a bar. The music varies, and it is sometimes booked out for events, so check before you go. Map 1 B2

Entertainment

A colourful capital of culture, Amsterdam offers everything from cabaret shows to comedy, as well as live music and concerts from classical to pop and rock.

Concerts & Live Music

Amsterdam is a great city for music. However, some venues are quite small and tickets go fast, so it's a good idea to keep an eye on publications such as *Amsterdam Weekly*, or websites like www.aub.nl to make sure you don't miss out. Paradiso (p.192) and Melkweg (p.192) are popular for rock and pop performances and often pull big names. They also get some great up-and-coming acts and the tickets are quite affordable.

Other venues which hold a wide range of musical events include the Concertgebouw, Muziektheater and Koninklijk Theater Carré. The Concertgebouw (Concertgebouwplein 2, Oud Zuid, 020 671 83 45) shows classical performances by artists from around the world. Het Muziektheater (Amstel 3, Centrum, 020 625 54 55)

Strip's Off

Amsterdam is well known for its tolerant approach to the sex industry, but a clean-up campaign has begun. Famous venues such as The Banana Bar are being closed down, with fashion designers snapping up the spaces previously occupied by prostitutes and cabarets.

is a startling modern structure that's lit up beautifully at night and is the home of the Netherlands Opera (www.dno.nl) and National Ballet. It also draws quality troupes from around the world. It's worth going to a concert at the Koninklijk Theater Carré (Amstel 112, 0900 252 5255) just to see the building.

For information on events in Amsterdam, the best source is the free *Uitkrant* published by the Amsterdam Uitburo (www.aub.nl). Its office is on Leidseplein and you can buy tickets for everything there and also online. Other sources of info include www.amsterdam.info/events, www.iamsterdam.nl and the national tourist board (www.holland.com).

Comedy

Boom Chicago (020 423 01 01, www.boomchicago.nl) perform a blend of improvisational comedy and social commentary. There are nightly shows at the 300 seat Leidseplein Theater (Map 9-B3), where you can also enjoy a meal with the performance. The shows are based on improvisation and involve audience suggestions and audience participation. Tickets cost around €20. You can get drinks during the show, including beer, wine and cocktails.

Casinos
Gambling isn't overly popular in the Netherlands, not surprising given the conservative, Calvinistic nature of the Dutch. There is only one legal casino chain, Holland Casino. The Amsterdam branch is located on Max Euweplein (see p.66).

Profile

Culture

Colourful history, artistic flair, freedom of expression and a cosmopolitan mix of people – Amsterdam's culture is rich, warm and welcoming.

Amsterdam packs a cultural punch disproportionate to its tiny size. Its rich heritage is not just visible in its canalside mansions or museums (though there are more of both of those per square kilometre than any other city in the world), but in the mindset of its citizens. There's that fabled reputation for tolerance stretching over centuries, which has attracted political exiles, religious refugees, artists, thinkers and rebels of all persuasions.

The city vibe is warm, relaxed and inclusive. Such an appealing melange, in fact, that some visitors never make it home. English is almost the second language but you'll find German and French spoken well too. Expat labour, particularly in the finance, service and creative industries, is a significant contributor to the economy. Amsterdam is unlike any other city in the Netherlands or indeed the world – 'a country by itself' as historian Geert Mak famously said.

People & Traditions

Clogs, windmills, cheese, tulips and diamonds are iconically associated with the Dutch, but cultural values might also make an impression. Conspicuous or attention-seeking behaviour generally will be frowned upon, and this is not– except maybe on Queen's Day (p.35) – a nation of exhibitionists.

A stall selling everything orange on Queen's Day

Dutch society is renowned for its tolerance, and social policies reflect this liberalism. This is very apparent as you explore the city, with the women in the windows of the Red Light District and the coffeeshops the most vivid examples of this progressivism. Whether it's abortion, euthanasia or religion, the culture here embraces the freedom of the individual.

The arts are taken seriously. Songs to accompany a more sentimental mood can sometimes be heard – you might hear a blast of Geef mij maar Amsterdam (Just give me Amsterdam) or Aan de Amsterdamse Grachten (On the Amsterdam Canals) coming from a Jordaan bar.

Although the Dutch are open and approachable, there's a punctilious approach to social arrangements. Meals, visits and other engagements are booked in advance; orderliness is important. The Dutch try to make life as gezellig (cosy, warm, comforting) as possible. Sipping a jenever in a snug bar while chatting to friends is very gezellig.

Food & Drink

The Dutch have a hard time with their 'traditional' culinary reputation which is often represented as cheese, more cheese and variations on a theme of mashed potatoes and cabbage.

Dutch food used to consist of straightforward, no-nonsense grub – lamb, pork or beef, potatoes (fried or boiled) and boiled cabbage, carrot or onion. Breakfast and lunch are largely interchangeable in terms of the types of food eaten, usually consisting of sandwiches of cheese, peanut butter (invented in Holland), jam, ham or salami. Unique to Holland is the use of chocolate or coloured sprinkles as a topping on bread – enjoyed by grownups as well as kids. At lunch, bread is served open-faced with a hearty dollop of salad, chopped into small pieces. Pannekoek (pancakes) have a variety of toppings, from sweet to savoury - favourites are syrup or powdered sugar toppings.

Maatjes haring (raw herring) is eaten covered with minced onions and sweet gherkins. Drop (liquorice candy) comes in both sweet and salty forms. Tostis are delectable toasted sandwiches filled with cheese and ham.

Over the years, former colonies have come to the rescue and Dutch citizens from Suriname, Indonesia and the Dutch Antilles have made their culinary mark with some surprising hybrids. Now Amsterdam's food really is international. Gourmet shops attract grateful customers and there are some great guides to local restaurants (try www.iens.nl and www. specialbite.nl), and see Going Out on p.162.

The Dutch are keen on sturdy fare, and snacks are also pretty solid. Popular options in bars or in fastfood chain Febo, are kroketten (tubes of

Proost!

Think Dutch beer and you think of the famous Heineken green bottles – the company is the world's second-largest brewer. As well as sampling it in the city's bars, you can also enjoy a trip to the Heineken Experience Museum (p.82). However, there are many other varieties of beer besides pils, including the darker bokbiers. Dutch gin (Jenever) was originally distilled for medical purposes but had a huge export market by the end of the 18th century.

pureed meat/potato) and bitterballen (round versions) which come with mustard for dunking. Vlaamse (Belgian) chips/frites come with various toppings (satay sauce, curry ketchup, mayo, onions). Go for patatas oorlog (war potatoes) and you get the lot.

Religion

The oldest building in Amsterdam is a church – the 14th century Oude Kerk (p.68) that was consecrated in 1306, but over the years the Netherlands has become increasingly secular. The most popular religion is Christianity, and Catholics (31%) are the biggest group. Until the 'Alteration' of 26 May 1578, Amsterdam was a Catholic city. When Protestant Calvinists took over, churches were stripped of their decorations and worship of other religions was banned.

Despite this, tolerance and liberty of thought ultimately prevailed and Amsterdam became the refuge for many immigrants fleeing their countries for religious and political reasons. Before and during the second world war this included Jews escaping the Nazis' anti-semitism, many of whom would later die in the death camps after the German Army invaded Holland.

With over a million practising Muslims, Islam is one of the country's main religions. By 2020, it is estimated that 7% of the population will be Muslim and 10% Catholic. Turks make up 80% of the Muslim minority. In Amsterdam, the diversity of worship reflects the city's multiculturalism. Protestant groups include Dutch Reformed and Reformed, Evangelical, Quaker, Pentecostal, Methodist and Charistmatic. There are

Konninklijk Paleis

also Buddhists, Hindus, humanists and members of other philosophical groups, as well as a Russian Orthodox Church.

Government & Politics

The Netherlands is a constitutional monarchy with a bicameral (two-chamber) parliament, called the Staten Generaal. Although Amsterdam is the capital, the Dutch parliament, government ministries and foreign embassies are all based in Den Haag (The Hague). Unusually, the monarch is part of the government, and Queen Beatrix (whose powers are mostly ceremonial) is the current head of state. The Dutch monarchy is referred to as being a 'cycling monarchy' because of its informal relationship with the public.

Centuries in the contained communities of the polders (pieces of land protected by dykes, under constant threat of flooding) have resulted in the Dutch becoming known for their planning, organisation and pursuit of consensus. This is reflected in the country's political structures, where the philosophy of the 'Poldermodel' endures. Dutch foreign policy is focused on international cooperation as the key to peace and prosperity.

Parliament consists of an upper chamber (eerste kamer) of 75 members elected by provincial councils every four years, and a lower chamber (tweede kamer) containing 150 members elected, also every four years, by proportional representation. Coalition cabinets are the norm. The last elections were in 2006 and saw swings to the Socialist Party (SP), a drop in support for the conservative VVD, and a fragmented vote split among the smaller parties such as the Green Left (GL) and right-wing Party for Freedom (PVV). The Party for Animals was the first animal rights organisation to win seats in a European parliament.

The political climate has heated up with the launch of Rita Verdonk's movement Trots op Nederland ('Proud of the Netherlands'). The ex-immigration minister is targeting her party at those disenchanted with the political system.

Top Development Nation

On the strength of its generous aid giving, falling greenhouse gas emissions and support for investment in developing countries, the Netherlands is top of *Foreign Policy* magazine's Commitment to Development Index 2006.

Clockwise from top left: Rembrandtsplein, St Urbanus Church, multicultural Amsterdam

History

The Golden Age changed the world, but the Dutch also endured occupation by the Nazis. Post-war society broke new ground with its liberalism.

For much of its early history Amsterdam was a boggy swamp. The area south of the Rhine was part of the Roman Empire (Pliny lived near Leiden) until the fifth century, and throughout the middle ages consisted of many separate feudal entities. Around 1270 the Amstel was dammed, and a village grew up on the site of what is now Dam Square. Aemstelledamme was granted its first charter in 1300 and by 1425 still only had a few houses and a church.

In 1452 the mostly wooden city was razed by fire, and only parts of the medieval architecture remain, such as the Munttoren (Mint Tower) in Muntplein. By the 1500s, when the Spanish branch of the House of Habsburg was the most potent force in Europe, the Low Countries, along with present day Belgium and Luxembourg, were part of the Holy Roman Empire of Charles V. Amsterdam prospered through trading, and by 1500 the city had grown to 9,000 inhabitants.

Eighty Years' War & Independence

Under King Philip II of Spain religious tensions came to the surface. The teachings of Calvin had taken hold and the Catholic king's persecution of Protestantism was regarded by the lowlanders as a restriction on religious freedom. Even Dutch Catholics were outraged by the antics of the Spanish

Inquisition. In 1568, the northern Dutch provinces revolted under Prince William of Orange, and so began a protracted battle for independence – the Eighty Years' War. This ended in 1648 with the Peace of Westphalia and recognition of the United Provinces as an independent state. William of Orange Nassau (Catholic, Lutheran, Father of The Fatherlands) took the position of Stadtholder (provincial governor).

Golden Age

Goods flowed into Amsterdam from all over the world, and people also poured into the city. The Dutch East India Company (VOC) was established in 1602 to coordinate shipping and trade with south-east Asia. Such was its global power, it could establish colonies, sign treaties and declare war. The Dutch West India Company (WIC) monopolised the seas between West Africa and the Americas and governed New Amsterdam which later became New York. William II and his son William III both married English princesses and the latter became King of England.

In 1609 the Bank of Amsterdam was founded and a huge influx of skilled immigrants led to industrial diversification. Jewish workers from Spain and Portugal brought diamonds, and the religious freedom of the republic attracted many immigrants as Amsterdam became a magnet for intellectual refugees such as Spinoza and Descartes.

The Dutch artists of this period – Rembrandt, Vermeer, Frans Hals – are universally known. The construction of the canal ring began in 1613, and by 1640 Amsterdam's population had risen to 139,000.

French Occupation

As the age of enlightenment spread across the rest of Europe, the 18th century saw a period of Dutch decline. The country's sea routes were under threat from the English and its lands from the French. There was a period of pro-French feeling with the Velvet Revolution and the establishment of the Batavian Republic, but the liberté, egalité and fraternité did not last long. In 1810 the Emperor Napoleon removed his brother from Amsterdam and incorporated the Netherlands into the French Empire, until its collapse in 1813.

By the time the Kingdom of the Netherlands was finally established in 1815 (it initially included Belgium), Amsterdam was struggling, but philanthropists like Samuel Sarphati (banks, construction, the Amstel Hotel) and Paul van Vlissingen (steamships and engineering) got the city moving again. Trams and bicycles arrived in the 1880s, and arts and architecture in Gothic, Renaissance and Baroque-inspired styles blossomed.

World Wars

During the first world war the Netherlands remained neutral, but by 1940 there was no protection from the German war machine and the country was occupied throughout the second world war. Exiled in London, Queen Wilhelmina spoke to her subjects through stirring broadcasts transmitted by the BBC. The round-up of the Jewish population began in 1941 and 76% were deported to concentration camps, with few survivors. Thousands of Amsterdam residents starved to death during the 'Hunger Winter' of 1944.

Post-War Prosperity & Changing Society

The resilient Dutch bounced back after the war, abandoning neutrality by signing up to NATO, the Treaty of Rome (one of six founder members of what become the EU) and a new economic grouping, Benelux. By 1948 they were able to celebrate the coronation of one Dutch housewife, Queen Juliana, and the athletic prowess of another (Fanny Blankers-Koen at the Olympics). Former colonies became independent: Indonesia (after a struggle) in 1949; Suriname much later in 1975. Generous social legislation ensured the 60s and 70s were colourful times. Hippies camped out in Amsterdam's Vondelpark, John Lennon and Yoko Ono had a 'bed-in' for world peace at the Hilton in 1969 and homosexuals found a spiritual home (same-sex marriage was legalised in 2001).

Amsterdam's population reached its peak in 1964 at almost 870,000. The government's approach to soft drugs and prostitution was 'pragmatic' and the Netherlands was seen (by its inhabitants as well as the outside world) as a glowing example of freedom and tolerance.

Immigration & Integration

The liberal image of Amsterdam has been shaken in recent years with controversial policies dealing with problems associated with rising immigration and non-integration. The murders of politician Pim Fortuyn and film director/cultural commentator Theo van Gogh shocked the world. The position of Islam and the integration of non-western foreigners remains one of the Netherlands' most debated issues.

Amsterdam Timeline

50BC-400AD	The Low Countries are part of the Roman Empire.
1300	Amsterdam is granted city rights.
1533	Birth of William of Nassau, Prince of Orange, founder of the Dutch Oranje-Nassau dynasty.
1602	The East India Company is founded, coinciding with the Dutch Golden Age.
1606	Birth of Rembrandt.
1613	Digging of the grachtengordel – Amsterdam's canal ring – begins.
1635	'Tulip Mania' (inflated prices for the flowers) strikes the country.
1815	Amsterdam becomes capital of the Netherlands.
1853	Birth of Van Gogh.
1900	Ajax football club formed.
1914-1918	The Dutch remain neutral during the first world war.
1940	German troops invade the Netherlands; Rotterdam is badly bombed.

1944	The Benelux agreement is signed by the Dutch, Luxembourg and Belgian governments.
1945	End of the occupation (8 May). Canadian soldiers free Amsterdam.
1947	Anne Frank's diary is published.
1948	Juliana becomes Queen.
1969	John and Yoko lie in bed for World Peace.
1975	Suriname gains independence.
1976	Decriminalisation of cannabis.
1980	Beatrix becomes Queen.
1986	Stopera (City Hall and Muziektheater) built.
1999	Prostitution legalised.
2001	Single-sex marriage given legal status.
2002	Introduction of the Euro. Goodbye Guilders.
2002	Right wing anti-immigration politician Pim Fortuyn is assassinated.
2005	Dutch voters reject proposed EU constitution.
2007	Jan Peter Balkenende is sworn in as head of a three-party coalition.

Amsterdam Today

Dutch personal freedoms are famous the world over, but managing multiculturalism is now the country's biggest challenge.

The Dutch Style Of Liberty

The city continues to attract the artists, students, rebels and renegades looking for the tolerance that Amsterdam is famous for. There is an extremely strong community of diverse cultural and ethnic groups; perhaps the best reflection of Amsterdam's liberal ethos was the city's celebration of its first legalised same-sex civil marriages in 2001.

Until the 1960s, society consisted of different 'pillars' (religious and political) which co-existed quite happily. But rapid secularisation and the most recent influx of immigration has triggered a huge debate about cultural identity and what it means (or could mean) to be Dutch. 'The characteristically Dutch form of liberty', said Amsterdam's mayor Job Cohen recently, 'involves more than just the freedom to express individual integrity; it also involves freedom from interference from others'. The latter, however, is disappearing and today's Dutch are unsure about how to deal with each other's freedoms. Anti-discrimination laws to ensure equal treatment (including for women and homosexuals) have long been part of the Netherlands' 'multidimensional liberty'.

Policies towards drugs, prostitution, religion, marriage, abortion, euthanasia and alternative lifestyles have generally added to the Dutch reputation for being relaxed but pragmatic.

Architectuurcentrum Amsterdam

Race Relations

Immigration and integration are resolutely on the political agenda in the Netherlands, particularly since the murders of anti-immigration politician Pim Fortuyn (2002) and controversial filmmaker Theo van Gogh (2004). Headlines such as 'Jihad behind the Dykes' or 'The Dutch Identity is Being Lost' do not speak of peaceful cohabitation or suggest a positive view of race relations. Amsterdam's mayor Job Cohen is pursuing integration policies for the city and favours an 'inclusive' approach to Dutch identity. He believes 'It is possible to be Dutch, and white, black, brown or yellow. It is possible to be Dutch, and white, secular and liberal. It is just as possible to be Dutch, and black, Muslim and conservative.'

New Developments

Recent years have seen the city authorities begin a major refurbishment of Amsterdam, which is only mid-way through. Unfortunately this means that occasionally the city can seem under construction, but this won't last for ever, and it is really only noticeable along the new North/South Metro line which is still being built.

The once medieval city has continued to expand and grow, most strikingly by developing the islands and harbour area, Zeeburg, (p.94) behind Centraal Station. This area, along with housing residential developments, is also home to some of the finest new architecture and cultural institutions in the city, offering an internationally renowned selection of music, theatre, art, photography, film, festivals, dance, and museums.

Clockwise from top left: bicycle locker, modern office buildings, Amsterdam World Trade Center

Maps

Map 1

Amsterdam Overview

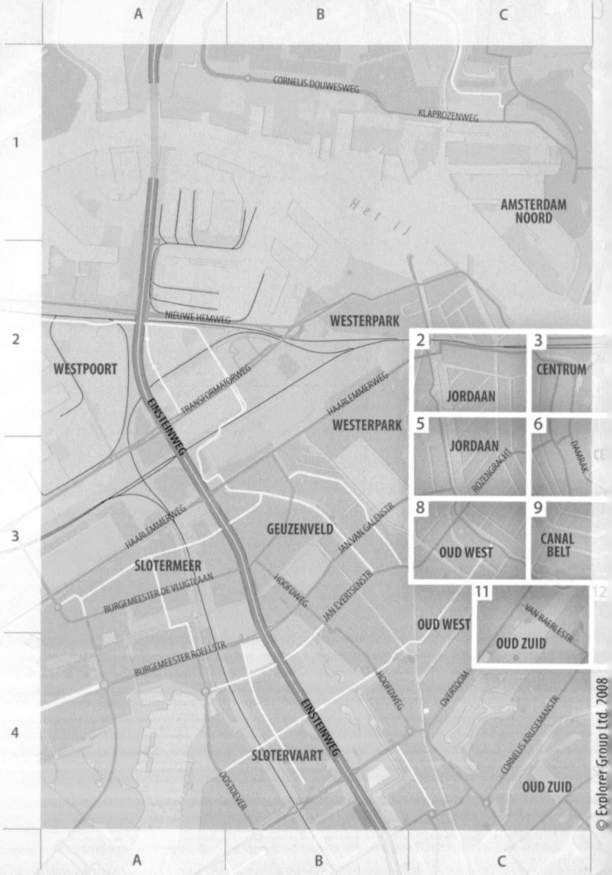

N

CORNELIS DOUWESWEG

KLAPROZENWEG

Het IJ

AMSTERDAM NOORD

NIEUWE HEMWEG

WESTERPARK

WESTPOORT

TRANSFORMATORWEG

EINSTEINWEG

HAARLEMMERWEG

WESTERPARK

HAARLEMMERWEG

GEUZENVELD

JAN VAN GALENSTR

SLOTERMEER

HOOFDWEG

JAN EVERTSENSTR

BURGEMEESTER DE VLUGTLAAN

BURGEMEESTER ROELLSTR

HOOFDWEG

EINSTEINWEG

OVERTOOM

SLOTERVAART

BOOTPLEIN

CORNELIS KRUSEMANSTR

2		3
JORDAAN		CENTRUM
5		6
JORDAAN		
	PRINSENGRACHT	DAMRAK
8		9
OUD WEST		CANAL BELT

11	12
	VAN BAERLESTR
OUD WEST	
OUD ZUID	

OUD ZUID

A   B   C

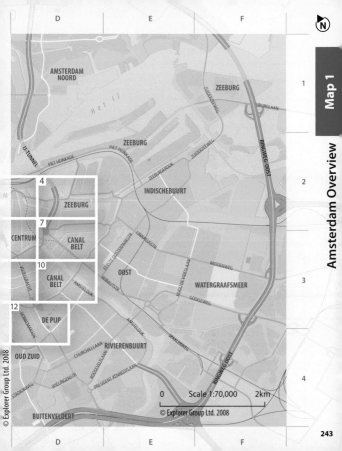

Map 1

Amsterdam Overview

AMSTERDAM NOORD

ZEEBURG

Het IJ

ZEEBURG

ZUIDERZEEWEG

IBURGLAAN

RINGWEG OOST

IJ-TUNNEL

PIET HEINKADE

PIET HEINKADE

ZEEBURGERDIJK

ZUIDERZEEWEG

INDISCHEBUURT

4

ZEEBURG

EERSTE OOSTERPARKSTR

LINNAEUSSTR

MIDDENWEG

7

CENTRUM

CANAL BELT

WIBAUTSTR

INSULINDEWEG

OOST

WATERGRAAFSMEER

10

CANAL BELT

AMSTELDIJK

GOOISEWEG

12

DE PIJP

NIEUWE AMSTEL

AMSTELDIJK

SPAKLERWEG

RINGWEG OOST

OUD ZUID

RIVIERENBUURT

CHURCHILLLAAN

BOERHAAVESTR

PRESIDENT KENNEDYLAAN

WEISPERACHT

STADIONWEG

WIELINGENSTR

0   Scale 1:70,000   2km

© Explorer Group Ltd. 2008

BUITENVELDERT

© Explorer Group Ltd. 2008

Legend

These maps include the most interesting parts of Amsterdam. Museums, galleries, restaurants, cafes, bars, shops and areas to explore are all marked with colour-coded symbols (see below).

You may also have noticed the large pull-out map at the back of the book. This is intended to give you an overview of the city. The perforated edges mean you can detach it from the main book, so you have even less to carry about with you. Or, if you and a travel companion have different plans for the day, you can take one each – so if one of you wants to soak up the culture, while the other wants to shop, there's no need for compromise.

00 Essentials **00 Exploring** **00 Sports & Spas** **00 Shopping** **00 Going Out**

Legend

H	Hotel		Land		Highway
mu	Museum/Heritage		Pedestrian Area		Major Road
+	Hospital		Built up Area/Building		Secondary Road
	Park/Garden		Industrial Area		Other Road
	Agriculture		Water	)= = ={	Tunnel
	Shopping		Cemetery	—O----	*Metro Station*
	Education	**†**	Church	—[]----	*Train Station*
	Stadium	**🛢**	Petrol Stations	(★)	Place of Interest
S105	Road Number	**DIEMEN**	Area Name	**ℹ**	Tourist Info
				✈	International Airport

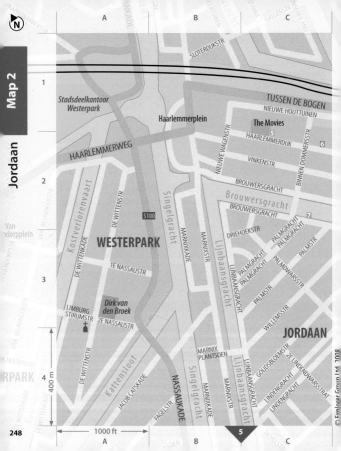

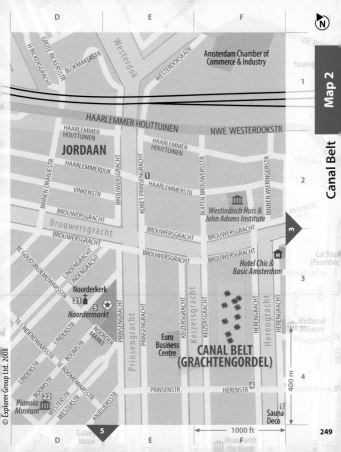

DE Pijp

Haveng

Amsterdam Chamber of
Commerce & Industry

1

HAARLEMMER HOUTTUINEN

NWE WESTERDOKSTR

HAARLEMMER
HOUTTUINEN

HAARLEMMER
HOUTTUINEN

JORDAAN

HAARLEMMERDIJK

HAARLEMMERSTR

DROOGBAK

VINKENSTR

BROUWERSGRACHT

2

Westindisch Huis &
John Adams Institute

BINNEN WIERINGERSTR

BROUWERSGRACHT

Brouwersgracht

BROUWERSGRACHT

BROUWERSGRACHT

3

BROUWERSGRACHT

BROUWERSGRACHT

BROUWERSGRACHT

Cat Boa
(Pozenbo

LINDENGRACHT

Hotel Chic &
Basic Amsterdam

3

LINDENGRACHT

Noorderkerk

21

5

Noordermarkt

NOORDER
MARKT

PRINSENGRACHT

PRINSENGRACHT

KEIZERSGRACHT

KEIZERSGRACHT

HERENGRACHT

HERENGRACHT

HERENGRACHT

Multatuli
Museum

KORSJESPOORTST

Euro
Business
Centre

**CANAL BELT
(GRACHTENGORDEL)**

4

Pianola
Museum

22

WESTERSTR

WESTERSTR

PRINSENSTR

HERENSTR

4

AUDWIJBURGWAL B

Sauna
Deco

1

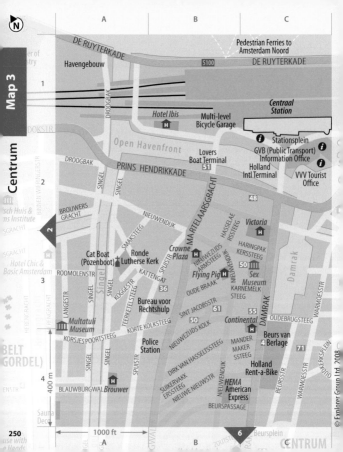

Map 3

Centrum

D E F

DE RUYTERKADE
DE RUYTERKADE

STATIONSPLEIN
STATIONSPLEIN

Districts
Postkantoor 45

Stedel
Museum 1

OOSTERDOKSKADE

Centraal
Station

Botel H

Canal Bus Dock

OOSTERDOKSKADE

Oosterdok

St Nicolaaskerk 12

OUDEZIJDS KOLK

57

CENTRUM 2

PRINS HENDR

NH Barbizon
Palace 29 H

GELDERSEKADE

KROMME WAAL

Grand Hotel
Amráth

H 5 PRINS HENDRIKKADE 4

51

Scheepvaarthuis

BINNENKAT

GELDERSEKADE

ZEEDIJK

Waalseilandsgracht 3

Ons' Lieve
Heer op
Solder 10

WAALSTEEG

BINNENKANT

The Crown H

KORTE NIEZEL

BINNEN BANTAMMERSTR

Museum
Amstelkring

NIEUWE
JONKERSTR

LASTAGEWEG

OUDE WAAL

48

NIEUWE RIDDERSTR

OOSTE
Montelbaanstore

Erotic
Museum

Guan
Yin Shrine

RECHT BOOMSSLOOT
RECHT BOOMSSLOOT

GELDERSEKADE

ZEEDIJK

Oude
Kerk

400 m

11 47
MOLENSTEEG

9

OUDEZIJDS

KONINGSSTR

KORTE KONIN
GSSTR

13

De Waag
Waterlooplein
Market 39

MONNIKENSTR

8

KORTE KEIZERSTR

Red Light
District
(De Wallen)

NIEUWMARKT

Nieuwmarkt

BLOEDSTR

Nieuwmarkt

4

The Bulldog H

The Shelter
City H

6

1000 ft

INBU
WER

251

ZEEBURG

Naval Officers'
Residences

Oosterdok

Stedelijk
Museum CS 43

OOSTDOKSKADE

IJ-TUNNEL

Oosterdok

NEMO 41

Vereniging
Museumhaven 5116

ARCAM 36

PRINS HENDRIKKADE

PRINS HENDRIKKADE

HENDRIKKADE

arthuis

BINNENKANT

CENTRUM

52

FOELIE
DWARSSTR

KADIJKSPLEIN

KALKMARKT

'S-GRAVENHEKJE

PEPERSTR

RAPENBURG

FOELIESTR

Police
Station

RAPENBURG

Brandweer
53

VALKENBURGERSTR

Spar

DE WAAL

OOSTERSEKADE

Montelbaanstoren 32

Entrepotdok

SCHIPPERSGRACHT

SLOOT
SLOOT

OUDESCHANS

NIEUWE UILENBURGERSTR

Uilenburgergracht

VALKENBURGERSTR

ANNE FRANKSTR

Nationaal
Vakbonds
Museum

TE KOLK

ERSSTR

PLANTA

4 m

400 m

1000 ft

252

BLENBLAER
WERE

A

STR

B

7

C

Sportsround

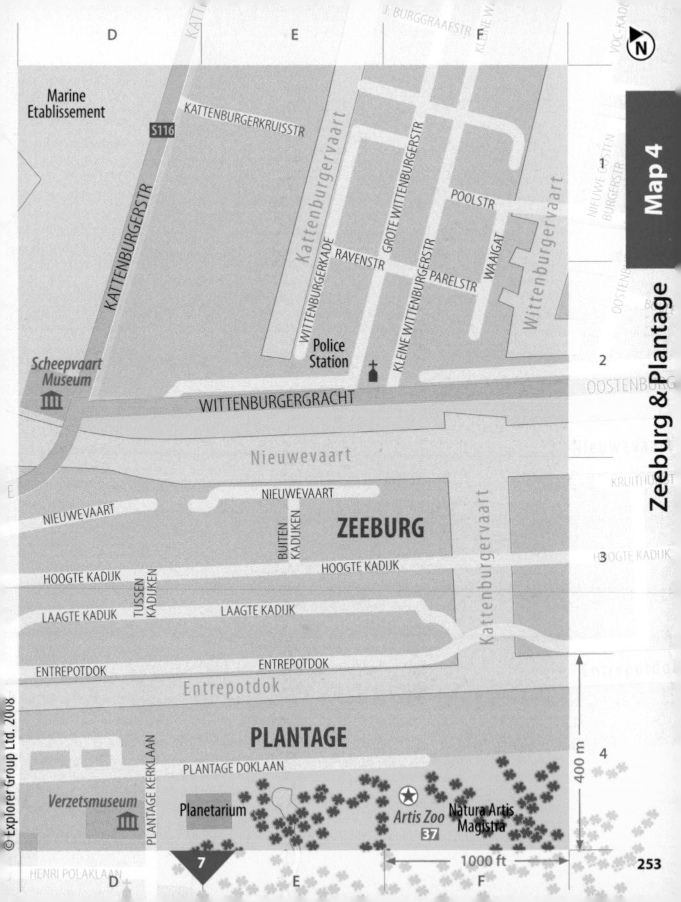

Map 4

Zeeburg & Plantage

D

E

F

J. BURGGRAAFSTR

KATT

KLEIN

VVC-KADE

N

Marine
Etablissement

S116

KATTENBURGERKRUISSTR

KATTENBURGERSTR

KATTENBURGERVAART

WITTENBURGERKADE

RAVENSTR

GROTE WITTENBURGERSTR

KLEINE WITTENBURGERSTR

POOLSTR

PARELSTR

WAAIGAT

WITTENBURGERVAART

NIEUWE

BURGERSTR

OOSTEN

1

Scheepvaart
Museum

Police
Station

2

OOSTENB

WITTENBURGERGRACHT

Nieuwevaart

KRUITHU

NIEUWEVAART

ZEEBURG

NIEUWEVAART

NIEUWEVAART

BUITEN
KADIJKEN

HOOGTE KADIJK

KATTENBURGERVAART

3

OGTE KADIJK

HOOGTE KADIJK

LAAGTE KADIJK

TUSSEN
KADIJKEN

LAAGTE KADIJK

ENTREPOTDOK

ENTREPOTDOK

Entrepotdok

ntrepotdok

PLANTAGE

PLANTAGE KERKLAAN

PLANTAGE DOKLAAN

400 m

4

Verzetsmuseum

Planetarium

Artis Zoo
37

Natura Artis
Magistra

HENRI POLAKLAAN

7

1000 ft

253

D

E

F

© Explorer Group Ltd. 2008

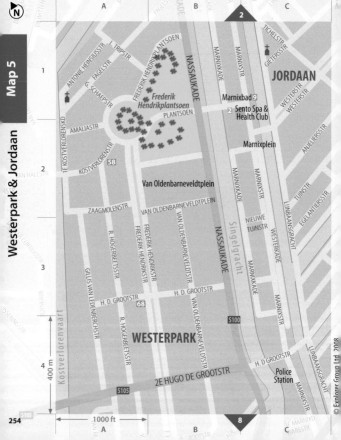

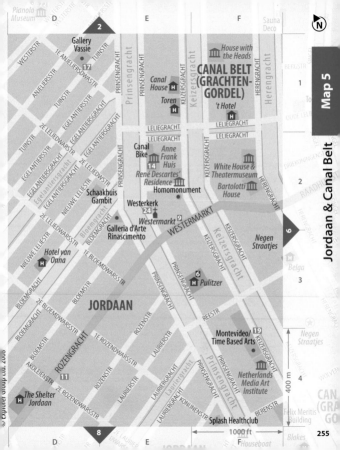

Map 5

Jordaan & Canal Belt

Pianola Museum

D

2

E

F

Sauna Deco

N

Gallery Vassie

17

WESTERSTR

1E ANJELIERSDWARSSTR

ANJELIERSGRACHT

TUINSTR

PRINSENGRACHT

PRINSENGRACHT

KEIZERSGRACHT

House with the Heads

BERGSTR

HERENGRACHT

CANAL BELT (GRACHTEN-GORDEL)

HERENGRACHT

To

1

OUDE LELI

TUINSTR

EGELANTIERSSTR

2E LELIEDWARSSTR

EGELANTIERSGRACHT

EGELANTIERSGRACHT

Canal House

Toren

H

H

't Hotel

H

LELIEGRACHT

LELIEGRACHT

LELIEGRACHT

LELIEGRACHT

2E LELIESTR

EGELANTIERSGRACHT

NIEUWE LELIESTR

PRINSENGRACHT

Canal Bike

14

Anne Frank Huis

KEIZERSGRACHT

HERENGRACHT

DRIEKONINGENSTR

RAADHUI

2

2E LELIEDWARSSTR

Schaakhuis Gambit

9

René Descartes' Residence

White House & Theatermuseum

Bartolotti House

NIEUWE LELIESTR

Westerkerk

Homomonument

HERENGRACHT

6

BLOEMGRACHT

BLOEMGRACHT

Galleria d'Arte Rinascimento

24

Westermarkt

WESTERMARKT

KEIZERSGRACHT

Negen Straatjes

Hotel van Onna

H

1E BLOEMDWARSSTR

BLOEMSTR

PRINSENGRACHT

H

Belga

2E BLOEMDWARSSTR

6

Pulitzer

H

3

BLOEMGRACHT

2E BLOEMDWARSSTR

JORDAAN

ROZENSTR

PRINSENGRACHT

REESTR

KEIZERSGRACHT

Negen Straatjes

BLOEMGRACHT

1E ROZENDWARSSTR

ROZENSTR

LAURIERSTR

Montevideo/ Time Based Arts

19

KEIZERSGRACHT

400 m

AKOLEIENSTR

11

2E ROZENDWARSSTR

ROZENSTR

LAURIERSTR

LAURIERGRACHT

PRINSENGRACHT

LAURIERGRACHT

Netherlands Media Art Institute

WUWEI

CAN (GRA GO

4

The Shelter Jordaan

H

1E LAURIER DWARS

KONINENSTR

BERENSTR

Felix Meritis Building

Splash Healthclub

© Explorer Group Ltd. 2008

D

8

E

1000 ft

F

Houseboat

Blakes

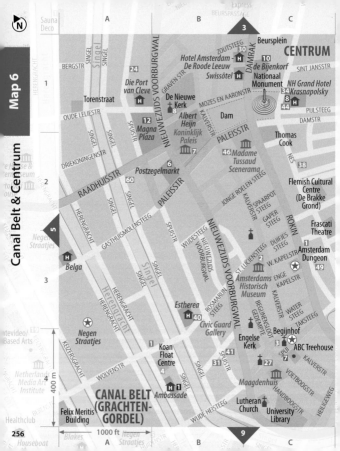

Map 6

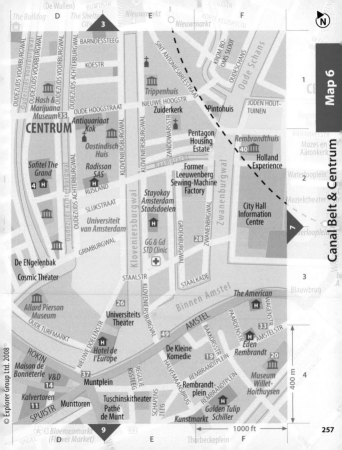

(De Wallen)

The Bulldog

The Sheltrex City

Nieuwmarkt

Nieuwmarkt

KORTE KEIZERSTR

KROM BO-OMS SLOOT

OUDESCHANS

Oude Schans

BARNDESSTEEG

KOESTR

OUDEZIJDS VOORBURGWAL

OUDEZIJDS VOORBURGWAL

OUDEZIJDS ACHTERBURGWAL

SINT ANTONIES-BREESTRAAT

NIEUWE HOOGSTR

JODEN HOUT-TUINEN

Hash & Marijuana Museum 35

OUDE HOOGSTRAAT

Trippenhuis

Zuiderkerk

Pintohuis

Antiquariaat Kok

CENTRUM

NIEUWE HOOGSTRAAT

ZANDDWARSSTR

Pentagon Housing Estate

Rembrandthuis 40

Mozes en Aaronkerk

Oostindisch Huis

KLOVENIERSBURGWAL

Former Leeuwenberg Sewing-Machine Factory

Holland Experience

Waterlooplein

Sofitel The Grand 4

Radisson SAS

RUSLAND

Raamgracht

ZWANENBURGWAL

Muziektheater

OUDEZIJDS ACHTERBURGWAL

SLIJKSTRAAT

Stayokay Amsterdam Stadsdoelen

City Hall Information Centre

Waterlooplein 7

Universiteit van Amsterdam

GROENBURGWAL

28

KLOVENIERSBURGWAL

GRIMBURGWAL

GG & Gd STD Clinic

De ENgelenbak

STAALKADE

Cosmic Theater

STAALSTR

Binnen Amstel

The American

Allard Pierson Museum

26

Universiteits Theater

KLOVENIERSBURGWAL

AMSTEL

WAGENSTR

PAARDENSTR

Eden Rembrandt

AMSTELSTR

33

OUDE TURFMARKT

49

Blauwbrug

ROKIN

NIEUWE DOELENSTR

Hotel de l'Europe

De Kleine Komedie

BAKKERSTR

19

Museum Willet-Holthuysen

20

Maison de Bonneterie

Y&D

14

37

Muntplein

REGULIERSSTEEG

Rembrandt-plein

REMBRANDTPLEIN

Kalvertoren

11

Munttoren

Tuschinskitheater

Pathé de Munt

SCHAPENSTEEG

HAVENMANBRUG

REMBRANDTPLEIN

Golden Tulip Schiller

SPUISTR

Bloemenmarkt (Flower Market) 9

22

Kunstmarkt

Thorbeckeplein

© Explorer Group Ltd. 2008

400 m

1000 ft

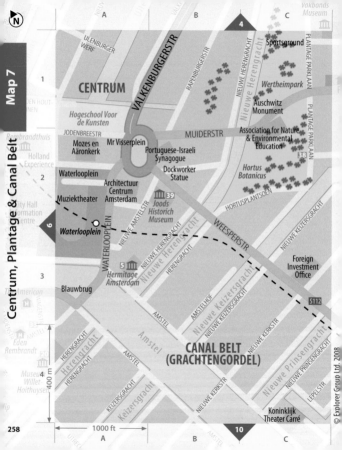

Map 7

Centrum, Plantage & Canal Belt

CENTRUM

ULENBURGER WERF

Hogeschool Voor de Kunsten

JODENBREESTR

Rembrandthuis

Holland Experience

Mozes en Aäronkerk

Waterlooplein

City Hall Information Centre

Muziektheater

6

Waterlooplein

Blaauwbrug

The American

Eden Rembrandt

Museum Willet Holthuysen

Mr Visserplein

Portuguese-Israeli Synagogue

Dockworker Statue

Architectuur Centrum Amsterdam

MUIDERSTR

Association for Nature & Environmental Education

Sportsground

Wertheimpark

Auschwitz Monument

Hortus Botanicus

38

Joods Historich Museum
39

Hermitage Amsterdam
5

HORTUSPLANTSOEN

WEESPERSTR

Foreign Investment Office

5112

Amstel

CANAL BELT (GRACHTENGORDEL)

HERENGRACHT

Herengracht

KEIZERSGRACHT

Keizersgracht

Nieuwe Keizersgracht

NIEUWE KEIZERSGRACHT

Nieuwe Herengracht

NIEUWE HERENGRACHT

AMSTEL

AMSTELHOF

NIEUWE KERKSTR

Nieuwe Kerkstr

Nieuwe Prinsengracht

NIEUWE PRINSENGRACHT

LEPCLSTR

Koninklijk Theater Carré

NIEUWE AMSTELSTR

WATERLOOPLEIN

VALKENBURGERSTR

RAPENBURGERSTR

NIEUWE HERENGRACHT

PLANTAGE PARKLAAN

PLANTAGE PARKLAAN

Vakbonds Museum

Utrecht

400 m

1000 ft

258

10

Map 7

PLANTAGE

CANAL BELT (GRACHTENGORDEL)

OOST

Verzetsmuseum

Planetarium

Artis Zoo

Natura Artis Magistra

Artis Geological Museum

Artisbibl

Aquarium

PLANTAGE MIDDENLAAN

Hotel Rembrandt

PLANTAGE MIDDENLAAN

Hollandsche Schouwburg

PLANTAGE MUIDERGRACHT

PLANTAGE MUIDERGRACHT

Plantage Muidergracht

Universiteit van Amsterdam

Kriterion Cinema

Weesperplein

© Explorer Group Ltd. 2008

PLANTAGE KERKLAAN

PLANTAGE WESTERMANLAAN

PLANTAGE WESTERMANLAAN

ROETERSSTR

NIEUWE KERKSTR

Nieuwe Prinsengracht

NIEUWE PRINSENGRACHT

NIEUWE ACHTERGRACHT

NIEUWE ACHTERGRACHT

NIEUWE ACHTERGRACHT

NIEUWE ACHTERGRACHT

VALCKENIERSTR

VALCKENIERSTR

SARPHATISTR

SPINOZASTR

SPINOZAHOF

Singelgracht

MAURITSKADE

VAN MUSSCHENBROEKSTR

A. CAMPERSTR

WEESPERSTR

Hotel

400 m

1000 ft

259

D E F

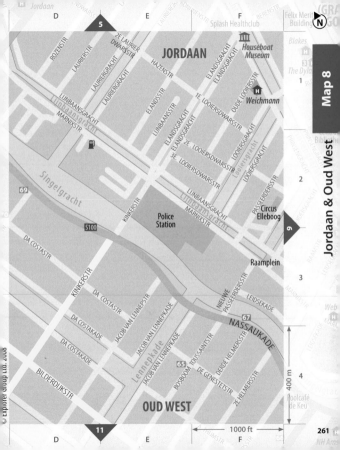

Map 8

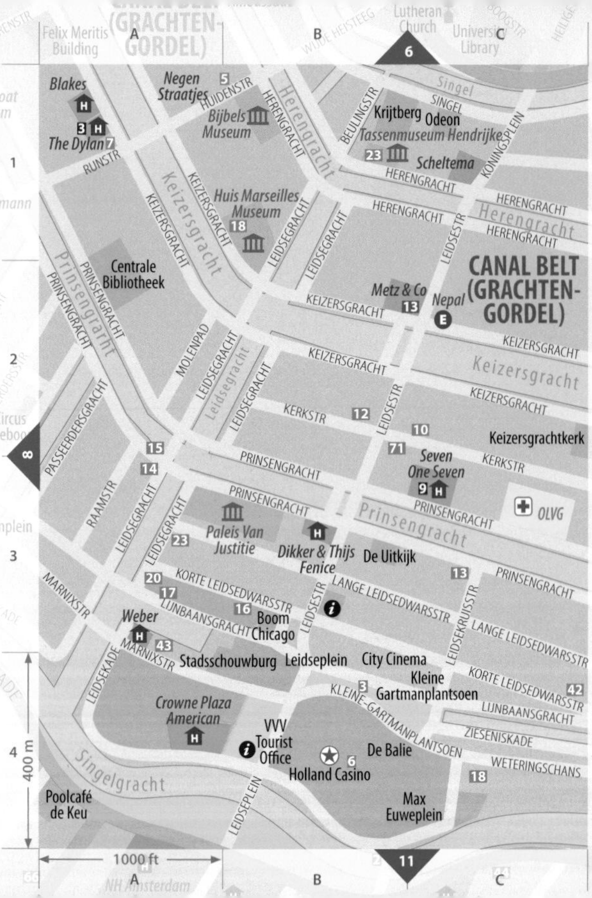

Map 9

Canal Belt

N

CANAL BEL
(GRACHTEN-
GORDEL)

Felix Meritis
Building

Lutheran
Church

Universi
Library

Singel

6

Blakes

Negen
Straatjes

5

Krijtberg Odeon

Tassenmuseum Hendrikje

3 The Dylan **7**

Bijbels
Museum

23 Scheltema

HUIDENSTR

BELLINGSTR

SINGEL

KONINGSPLEIN

HERENGRACHT

HERENGRACHT

Huis Marseilles
Museum

18

HERENGRACHT

Herengracht

HERENGRACHT

Centrale
Bibliotheek

KEIZERSGRACHT

Metz & Co

13

Nepal

E

CANAL BELT
(GRACHTEN-
GORDEL)

KEIZERSGRACHT

Keizersgracht

PRINSENGRACHT

MOLENPAD

LEIDSEGRACHT

KEIZERSGRACHT

KERKSTR

12

LEIDSESTR

10

Keizersgrachtkerk

2

KERKSTR

Circus
Elleboog

8

PASSEERDERSGRACHT

Seven
One Seven

7 **1**

9 **H**

+ OLVG

15

RAAMSTR

14

PRINSENGRACHT

PRINSENGRACHT

Prinsengracht

PRINSENGRACHT

LEIDSEGRACHT

23

Paleis Van
Justitie

Dikker & Thijs
Fenice

H

De Uitkijk

LANGE LEIDSEDWARSSTR

LEIDSEDWARSSTR

LANGE LEIDSEDWARSSTR

13

LEIDSEKRUISSTR

PRINSENGRACHT

MARNIXSTR

20

17

16

KORTE LEIDSEDWARSSTR

3

i

KORTE LEIDSEDWARSSTR

LEIDSESTR

Weber

LIJNBAANSGRACHT

Boom
Chicago

42

H

43

Stadsschouwburg

Leidseplein

City Cinema

Kleine
Gartmanplantsoen

LIJNBAANSGRACHT

NASSAUKADE

MARNIXSTR

LEIDSEKADE

KLEINE-GARTMANPLANTSOEN

3

Crowne Plaza
American

H

VVV
Tourist
Office

i

6

De Balie

ZIESENISKADE

18

WETERINGSCHANS

4 400 m

Singelgracht

Poolcafé
de Keu

Holland Casino

Max
Euweplein

LEIDSEPLEIN

LEIDSEPLEIN

1000 ft

NH Amsterdam

11

A **B** **C**

Map 9

Canal Belt

Munttoren
Tuschinskitheater Pathé
Kunstmarkt
Golden Tulip Schiller

SPUISTR
D
E
F

N

6
22

Bloemenmarkt
(Flower Market)

SINGEL

Banks
Mansion
H

Thorbeckeplein

VIJZELSTR

23
25

REGULIERSDWARSSTR

21

HERENGRACHT

Kattenkabinet

HERENGRACHT

Seven
Bridges
H

REGULIERSGRACHT

REGULIERSBREESTRAAT

HERENGRACHT

Herengracht

HERENGRACHT

Geelvinck
Hinlopen Huis

1

HERENGRACHT

Galerie Lieve
Hemel

Goethe
Institut

ABN-AMRO
Bank

FOAM

16

KEIZERSGRACHT

Herman
Brood
Gallery

27

De Appel

25

KEIZERSGRACHT

Keizersgracht

KEIZERSGRACHT

Amst
Ar

De

2

KEIZERSGRACHT

VIJZELSTR

Museum
Van Loon

KERKSTR

Hans Brinker
Budget
H

Kunsthandel
Peter Pappot

29

Jaski Art
Gallery

59

NIEUWE SPIEGELSTR

KERKSTR

CANAL BELT
(GRACHTENGORDEL)

PRINSENGRACHT

Prinsengracht

PRINSENGRACHT

10

NIEUWE LOOIERSSTR

NOORDERHE

BEULINGHE

PRINSENGRACHT

PRINSENGRACHT

NOORDERSTR

3

VIJZELGRACHT

NIEUWE LOOIERSDSTR

FOKKE SIMONSZSTR

WETERINGSTR

Galerie
Delaive

26

1E WETERINGDWARSSTR

2E WETERINGDWARSSTR

3E WETERINGDWARSSTR

NIEUWE WETERINGSTR

NIEUWE LOOIERSSTR

FOKKE SIMONSZSTR

LIJNBAANSGRACHT

4

SPIEGELGRACHT

45

31

Reflex Modern Art Gallery

WETERINGSCHANS

Lijnbaansgracht

400 m

12
D
Canal Bike
E
SINGELG

1000 ft

263

© Explorer Group Ltd. 2006

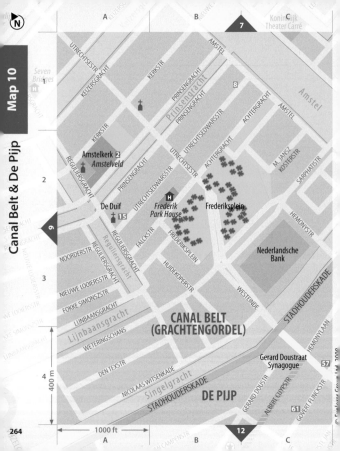

Map 10

Canal Belt & De Pijp

N

7

KONINKRIJK
Theater Carré

Seven
Bridges
1

UTRECHTSESTR

KEIZERSGRACHT

KERKSTR

AMSTEL

PRINSENGRACHT

PRINSENGRACHT

8

ACHTERGRACHT

AMSTEL

Amstel

KERKSTR

PRINSENDWARSSTR

UTRECHTSEDWARSSTR

UTRECHTSESTR

ACHTERGRACHT

M. JANSZ
KOSTERSTR

SAPHATISTR

Amstelkerk 2
Amstelveld

REGULIERSGRACHT

PRINSENGRACHT

2

De Duif

15

UTRECHTSEDWARSSTR

H
Frederik
Park House

Frederiksplein

HEMONYSTR

9

REGULIERSGRACHT

FALCKSTR

FREDERIKSPLEIN

Nederlandsche
Bank

NOORDERSTR

REGULIERSGRACHT

HUIDEKOPERSTR

3

NIEUWE LOOIERSTR

WESTEINDE

STADHOUDERSKADE

FOKKE SIMONSZSTR

LIJNBAANSGRACHT

Lijnbaansgracht

WETERINGSCHANS

CANAL BELT
(GRACHTENGORDEL)

HEMONYLAAN

Gerard Doustraat
Synagogue

57

4   400 m

DEN TEXSTR

NICOLAAS WITSENKADE

Singelgracht

STADHOUDERSKADE

DE PIJP

GERARD DOUSTR

ALBERT CUYPSTR

GOVERT FLINCKSTR

61

1000 ft

12

A   B   C

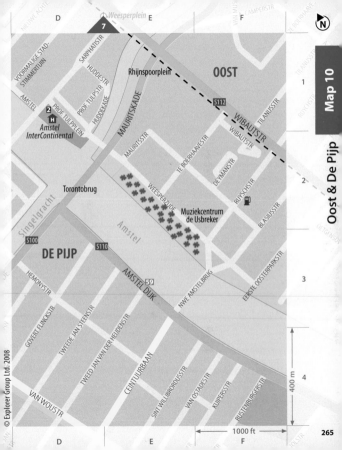

Map 10

Oost & De Pijp

D

E

F

○ Weesperplein

7

N

VOORMALIGE STAD-STIMMERTUIN

NIEUWE ACHTE

SARPHATISTR

HUDDESTR

Rhijnspoorplein

OOST

VAN MUS

TE KAMPERSTR

TE BOURHAA

TE OORHAAVE

AMSTEL

PROF. TULPSTR

HUDDEKADE

1

2

Amstel InterContinental

H

PROF. TULPPLEIN

MAURITSKADE

MAURITSSTR

1E BOERHAAVESTR

S112

WIBAUTSTR

WIBAUTSTR

TILANUSSTR

BURGSTR

Torontobrug

Singelgracht

WEESPERZIJDE

DEYMANSTR

BUSKENSTR

BUSCHSTR

BLASIUSSTR

2

Amstel

Muziekcentrum de IJsbreker

EERSTE OOSTERPARKSTR

WTGANSDWDR

S100

DE PIJP

S110

AMSTEL DIJK

59

NWE AMSTELBRUG

3

HEMONYSTR

GOVERT FLINCKSTR

TWEEDE JAN STEENSTR

TWEED JAN VAN DER HEIJDENSTR

CEINTUURBAAN

SINT WILLIBRORDUSSTR

VAN OSTADESTR

KUIPERSSTR

RUSTENBURGERSTR

400 m

4

VAN WOUSTR

1000 ft

D

E

F

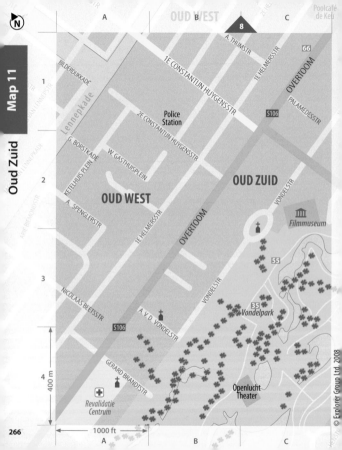

OUD WEST

Poolcafé
de Keti

8

A. THIJMSTR

1E CONSTANTIJN HUYGENSSTR

1E HELMERSSTR

66

OVERTOOM

BILDERDIJKKADE

1

PALAMEDESSTR

Lennepkade

2E CONSTANTIJN HUYGENSSTR

Police
Station

S106

VAN LENNEPKADE

G. BORSTKADE

W. GASTHUISPLEIN

OUD ZUID

KETELHUIS PLEIN

VONDELSTR

2

A. SPENGLERSTR

OUD WEST

Filmmuseum

ANJE BIELANDSTR

1E HELMERSSTR

OVERTOOM

55

VONDELSTR

3

NICOLAAS BEETSSTR

35

Vondelpark

A. V. D. VONDELSTR

S106

Openlucht
Theater

GERARD BRANDTSTR

4

400 m

Revalidatie
Centrum

1000 ft

© Explorer Group Ltd. 2008

A   B   C

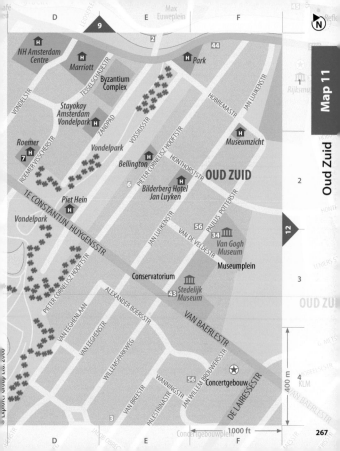

D · E · F

9

2

44

N

Map 11

Oud Zuid

1

Rijksmu

2

12

3

OUD ZU

4

KLM

267

D · E · F

NH Amsterdam Centre

Marriott

Byzantium Complex

Vondelstr

Tesselschadestr

Stayokay Amsterdam Vondelpark

Zandpad

Vossiusstr

Park

Hobbemastr

Jan Luijkenstr

Museumzicht

Roemer

Vondelpark

7

Roemer Visscherstr

Bellington

Pieter Cornelisz Hooftstr

Honthorststr

OUD ZUID

6

Bilderberg Hotel Jan Luyken

Piet Hein

1e Constantijn Huygensstr

Vondelpark

Jan Luijkenstr

Van de Veldestr

56

Paulus Potterstr

34

Van Gogh Museum

Museumplein

Pieter Cornelisz Hooftstr

Conservatorium

Alexander Boersstr

43

Stedelijk Museum

Van Eeghenlaan

Van Eeghenstr

Willemsparkweg

Van Breestr

Palestrinastr

Waningstr

Jan Willem Brouwersstr

56

Concertgebouw

VAN BAERLESTR

DE LAIRESSESTR

400 m

3

Jacob Obrec

Concertgebouwplein

1,000 ft

© Lonely Planet Ltd. 2008

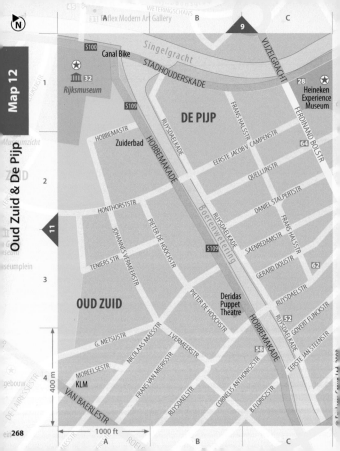

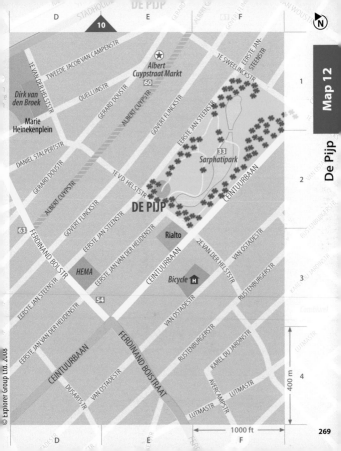

Map 12

De Pijp

N

D · E · F

STADHOU

DE PIJP

VAN WOUSTR

10

GERARD G

GUL

VAN WOUSTR

TWEEDE JACOB VAN CAMPENSTR

TE VAN DER HELSTSTR

Dirk van
den Broek

QUELLIJNSTR

GERARD DOUSTR

Albert
Cuypstraat Markt

60

ALBERT CUYPSTR

GOVERT FLINCKSTR

TE SWEELINCKSTR

EERSTE JAN-
STEENSTR

EERSTE JAN STEENSTR

1

Marie
Heinekenplein

DANIEL STALPERTSTR

GERARD DOUSTR

ALBERT CUYPSTR

TE V.D. HELSTSTR

Sarphatipark

33

CEINTUURBAAN

2

63

GOVERT FLINCKSTR

DE PIJP

EERSTE JAN STEENSTR

Rialto

FERDINAND BOLSTR

HEMA

EERSTE JAN VAN DER HEIJDENSTR

CEINTUURBAAN

2E VAN DER HELSTSTR

VAN OSTADESTR

Bicycle H

3

54

VAN OSTADESTR

RUSTENBURGERSTR

EERSTE JAN STEENSTR

EERSTE JAN VAN DER HEIJDENSTR

CEINTUURBAAN

FERDINAND BOLSTRAAT

VAN OSTADESTR

RUSTENBURGERSTR

KAREL DU JARDINSTR

AVERCAMPSTR

LUTMASTR

400 m

4

DUSARTSTR

LUTMASTR

LUTMASTR

1000 ft

D · E · F

Explorer
Products

Residents' Guides

All you need
to know about
living, working
and enjoying life
in these exciting
destinations

Abu Dhabi
Amsterdam
Bahrain
Barcelona
Beijing
Berlin
Dubai
Dublin
Geneva
Hong Kong
Kuala Lumpur
Kuwait
London
Los Angeles
New York
New Zealand
Oman
Paris
Qatar
Shanghai
Singapore
Sydney
Tokyo
Vancouver

Coming in 2008/9: Bangkok, Brussels, Mexico City, Moscow,
San Francisco, Saudi Arabia and Taipei

Mini Visitors' Guides

Perfect pocket-sized visitors' guides

Coming in 2008/9: Bangkok, Brussels, Mexico City, Moscow, San Francisco and Taipei

Activity Guides

Drive, trek, dive and swim... life will never be boring again

Check out www.explorerpublishing.com/products

Mini Maps

Fit the city in your pocket

Coming in 2008/9: Ajman, Al Ain, Bangkok,
Brussels, Fujairah, Mexico City, Moscow,
Ras Al Khaimah, San Francisco, Taipei,
Umm Al Quwain

Maps

Wherever you are, never get lost again

Explorer Team

Publishing
Publisher Alistair MacKenzie
Associate Publisher Claire England
Assistant to Associate Publisher
Kathryn Calderon

Editorial
Group Editor Jane Roberts
Lead Editors David Quinn, Katie Drynan,
Sean Kearns, Tim Binks, Tom Jordan
Deputy Editors Jakob Marsico, Jenny
Lyon, Pamela Afram, Richard Greig
Online Editor Helen Spearman
Senior Editorial Assistant
Mimi Stankova
Editorial Assistants
Grace Carnay, Ingrid Cupido

Design
Creative Director Pete Maloney
Art Director Ieyad Charaf
Design Manager Alex Jeffries
Junior Designer Jessy Perera
Layout Manager Jayde Fernandes
Designers Hashim M.M., Rafi VP,
Shawn Jackson Zuzarte
Cartography Manager
Zainudheen Madathil
Cartographers Juby Jose,
Noushad Madathil, Sunita Lakhiani
Traffic Manager Maricar Ong
Production Coordinator Joy Tubog

Photography
Photography Manager Pamela Grist
Photographer Victor Romero
Image Editor Henry Hilos

IT
IT Administrator Ajay Krishnan
Senior Software Engineer
Bahrudeen Abdul Kareem

Sales & Marketing
Media Sales Area Managers
Laura Zuffa, Paul Santer,
Pouneh Hafizi, Stephen Jones
International Media Sales Manager
Peter Saxby
Corporate Sales Area Manager
Ben Merrett
Corporate Sales Executive
Hannah Brisby
Marketing Manager Kate Fox
Marketing Executive Annabel Clough
Marketing Assistant Shedan Ebona
Digital Content Manager
Derrick Pereira
International Retail Sales Manager
Ivan Rodrigues
Business Relations Manager
Shyrell Tamayo
Retail Sales Coordinator
Sobia Gulzad
Retail Sales Supervisor Mathew Samuel
Retail Sales Merchandisers
Johny Mathew, Shan Kumar
Sales & Marketing Coordinator
Lennie Mangalino
Distribution Executives
Ahmed Mainodin, Firos Khan
Warehouse Assistant Najumudeen K.I.
Drivers Mohammed Sameer,
Shabsir Madathil

Finance & Administration
HR & Administration Manager
Marit Visser
Finance Manager Michael Samuel
Junior Accountant Cherry Enriquez
Accounts Assistant Darwin Lovitos
Administrators
Enrico Maullon, Kelly Tesoro
Drivers Rafi Jamal, Mannie Lugtu

Photography Books

Beautiful cities caught through the lens

Lifestyle Products & Calendars

The perfect accessories for a buzzing lifestyle

Check out www.explorerpublishing.com/products

Contact Us

▶ **Reader Response**
If you have any comments and suggestions, fill out
our online reader response form and you could win prizes.
Log on to **www.explorerpublishing.com**

▶ **Newsletter**
If you would like to receive the Explorer newsletter packed with
special offers, latest books updates and community news please
send an email to **marketing@explorerpublishing.com**

▶ **General Enquiries**
We'd love to hear your thoughts and answer any questions
you have about this book or any other Explorer product.
Contact us at **info@explorerpublishing.com**

▶ **Careers**
If you fancy yourself as an Explorer, send your CV (stating the
position you're interested in) to **jobs@explorerpublishing.com**

▶ **Designlab and Contract Publishing**
For enquiries about Explorer's Contract Publishing arm and
design services contact **designlab@explorerpublishing.com**

▶ **Maps**
For cartography enquries, including orders and comments,
contact **maps@explorerpublishing.com**

▶ **Corporate Sales**
For bulk sales and customisation options, for this book or any
Explorer product, contact **sales@explorerpublishing.com**

EXPLORER